The Guide to Critical Thinking
in Economics

Richard L. Epstein
Carolyn Kernberger
Advanced Reasoning Forum

THOMSON

SOUTH-WESTERN

Australia · Canada · Mexico · Singapore · Spain · United Kingdom · United States

THOMSON

SOUTH-WESTERN

The Guide to Critical Thinking in Economics
Richard L. Epstein/Carolyn Kernberger

Vice President/Editorial Director:
Jack Calhoun

Vice President/Editor-in-Chief:
Michael P. Roche

Publisher:
Michael B. Mercier

Senior Acquisitions Editor:
Peter Adams

Developmental Editor:
Steven Joos

Senior Production Editor:
Elizabeth A. Shipp

Executive Marketing Manager:
Janet Hennies

Senior Marketing Coordinator:
Jenny Fruechtenicht

Senior Media Technology Editor:
Vicky True

Media Developmental Editor:
Peggy Buskey

Media Production Editor:
Pam Wallace

Manufacturing Coordinator:
Sandee Milewski

Cover Designer:
Bethany Casey

Cover Image:
© PhotoDisc, Inc.

Printer:
Von Hoffmann Graphics

Names, characters, and incidents relating to any of the characters in this text are used fictitiously, and any resemblance to actual persons, living or dead, is entirely coincidental.

The moral rights of the authors have been asserted.

Critical Thinking in Economics

Richard L. Epstein and Carolyn Kernberger

Preface

Preface

When economists reason, they make arguments, they deduce from hypotheses, they create models, they offer explanations. There are reasonably clear standards of evaluation for those ways of reasoning, standards and skills we can master and use in our studies and work.

Critical thinking is evaluating whether we should be convinced that some claim is true or some argument is good, as well as formulating good arguments. This book is meant to help you learn the basic skills of critical thinking and apply them to the study of economics.

Those skills are the same ones we need in order to be able to reason well in our everyday life. Some methods, though, are specific to economics and the sciences or are done more carefully by economists. The examples from economics and science that we work through here allow us to see those methods more clearly. They do not assume any background beyond what you might be learning in a first-year introduction to economics. Examples from current economics textbooks are placed in quotation marks.

Critical thinking, though, is more than knowing definitions and rules and a few examples. It requires judgment developed through practice. You can find lots of examples, exercises, discussions, and practice for writing good arguments in our textbooks *Critical Thinking* and *Science Workbook for Critical Thinking*. Use this *Guide* as a place to start learning how to reason well. Your practice can come from analyzing the examples here and using these ideas in studying economics, reading the newspaper, working at your job, and talking with your friends and family.

This *Guide* is not meant to teach you how to think like an economist—that's the goal of your economics courses. What we hope to do here is to make it easier to understand those courses and see the assumptions and techniques that economists use in their reasoning.

The scientist thinks that he (or she, or whatever), of all people, has discovered something about how the universe behaves. So:

- Is this scientist right—and what does "right" mean, anyway?

- Can you think of even one different explanation that works as well or better?

- Did the test really, really, truly, unquestionably, completely test what the author thought he was testing?

- Is the scientist ruthlessly honest with himself about how well his idea explains everything, or could he be suffering from wishful thinking?

Annals of Improbable Research

It is this kind of questioning, backed by tools of analysis, that should become second nature by studying this *Guide*.

Dedicated to my parents, whose continual fostering of intellectual curiosity made possible my contributions to this book—C.K.

1   Claims

What are we arguing about? Is it a claim that is true or false, or is it just nonsense? Is it a claim whose truth is relative to what someone thinks, or is its truth-value independent of people? What standards are being invoked? These are the most fundamental questions we must answer before we can begin any analysis of reasoning. Section 1.1 is devoted to the nature of claims.

It doesn't help us to arrive at any better understanding of the world if we use words without knowing what they mean. But how do we know when we understand technical words correctly? In Section 1.2 we study how to make and recognize good definitions.

Before we turn to the nature of arguments, we'll look at ways people try to convince us without reasoning. In Section 1.3 we look at how claims can be concealed by manipulation of language, using loaded questions and other slanters.

1.1 Claims

We want to arrive at truths from our reasoning. So we need to be able to recognize whether a sentence is true or false and what kind of standards it invokes—or whether it is just nonsense.

> **Claim**   A claim is a declarative sentence used in such a way that it is either true or false (but not both).

Example 1   Dogs are mammals.
> *Analysis*   This is a claim.

Example 2 $2 + 2 = 5$
> *Analysis*   This is a claim, a false claim.

Example 3   Consumers want cheaper vacuum cleaners.
> *Analysis*   This is a claim.

Example 4   How can anyone be so dumb as to think that a managed economy is efficient?
> *Analysis*   This is not a claim. Questions are not claims, even if meant to be taken rhetorically.

Example 5   I wish I could get a job.
> *Analysis*   Whether this is a claim depends on how it's used. If Maria, who's been trying to get a job for three weeks says this to herself, it's not a claim—we don't say that a wish is true or false. On the other hand, if Dick's parents are berating him for not getting a job, he might say, "It's not that I'm not trying. I wish I could get a job." Since he could be lying, in that context it is a claim.

A basic divide in claims is between those that are about the world outside our minds and those that are about mental states.

> **Subjective and objective claims**   A claim is **subjective** if whether it is true or false depends on what someone (or something or some group) thinks, believes, or feels. A subjective claim invokes **personal standards**. Claims that are not subjective are **objective**, and those use **impersonal standards**.

Example 6   All economics professors are men.
> *Analysis*   This is an objective claim. It is false.

Example 7   The dogs in that advertisement prefer Bow-Wow Biscuits.
> *Analysis*   This is a subjective claim. Whether it is true depends on what the dogs *feel*.

Example 8   Inflation was 3.2% last year.

   Analysis   This is an objective claim. You can check government statistics to see whether it's true or false.

Example 9   I think that inflation was 3.2% last year.

   Analysis   This is a subjective claim. It need not have the same truth-value as Example 8.

Example 10   Investors in 1997 overwhelmingly preferred no-load mutual funds.

   Analysis   This is a subjective claim: whether it is true or false depends on what a group of people *thought*.

Example 11   Investors in 1997 invested more than twice as much money in no-load mutual funds as in other mutual funds.

   Analysis   This is an objective claim: whether it is true or false depends on how people *acted*.

It might seem that objective claims are ones whose truth-value we can check. But "There are an even number of stars in the sky" is objective, and no one knows how to check whether that's true or false. On the other hand, when our dog comes up to us shivering and wet in the middle of the winter, we can be very sure "Our dog is cold" is true. Whether a claim is objective or subjective only tells us what evidence to look for in determining its truth-value. So it's a serious error to mistake whether a claim is subjective or objective.

Example 12   Maria: Red is an ugly color for our company logo.

   Fernando: You're crazy. It's really beautiful.

   Analysis   This is an example of taking a subjective claim and treating it as objective. What's ugly to one person may be beautiful to another, so it's silly for Maria and Fernando to argue here.

Example 13   Maria: I deserve a raise—I did everything you said I should and I've been here two years like the company requires.

   Boss: That's just your opinion.

   Analysis   Maria has a tough time ahead of her, because her boss is taking an objective claim and treating it as subjective.

Throughout this text we'll often point out common mistakes in reasoning and label them *fallacies*. Here's one.

Subjectivist fallacy   It's a mistake to argue that because there is a lot of disagreement about whether a claim is true, it's therefore subjective.

Example 14   Socialism is the most efficient way to ensure that all members of a society are fed and clothed.

   Analysis   There's a lot of disagreement about this. But it's still objective, assuming "efficient" has been clearly defined.

Some sentences may look like claims, or people try to pass them off as claims, but they're worthless for reasoning. If we can't understand what someone is saying, we can't investigate whether it's true or false.

> **Vague sentence**   A sentence is vague if there are so many ways to understand it we can't settle on any one of those without the speaker making it clearer.

Example 15 Our dish soap is new and improved.
    Analysis This is too vague to be a claim.

Example 16 People who are disabled are just as good as people who aren't.
    Analysis This is too vague to be a claim: just as good in what way?

Yet everything we say is somewhat vague. After all, no two people have identical perceptions, and since the way we understand words depends on our experience, we all understand words a little differently. The issue isn't whether a sentence is vague, but whether it's *too vague*, given the context, for us to be justified in saying it has a truth-value.

Example 17 You say, "My economics professor showed up late for class on Tuesday."
    Analysis Which Tuesday? Who's your economics professor? What do you mean by "late"? 5 minutes? 30 seconds? How do you determine when she showed up? When she walked through the door? At exactly what point? When her nose crossed the threshold? That's silly. We all know "what you meant." This is not too vague in this context.

Example 18 Dick: It's cold outside.
    Analysis This is too vague to be an objective claim. What's cold? In parts of Brazil they say it's cold when it gets down to 68° F (20° C). But if it's meant as "It's too cold outside *for me*," then it's a perfectly good subjective claim.

A particular kind of vagueness is when there are just two or a very few ways to understand a sentence; we call those sentences **ambiguous**.

Example 19 Zoe saw the waiter with the glasses.
    Analysis This is ambiguous. Does it mean that Zoe saw with her eyeglasses, or that the waiter had eyeglasses, or was the waiter carrying drinking glasses? Perhaps in context we could tell which of these was meant.

Example 20 People in the average family in the U.S. spend $30 on entertainment every week.
    Analysis This is an example of a common kind of ambiguity: *between the group and the individual*. Does it mean that each family spends $30 or each member of the family spends $30? There is the same problem with evaluating "Dr. E's dogs eat over 10 pounds of meat every week." Does that mean each dog eats that much (big dog!) or do they together eat more than 10 pounds?

Whether a sentence is an objective claim, a subjective claim, or too vague to be taken as a claim may depend on what standards are being invoked.

Example 21 Harry says, "New cars today are really expensive."
    Analysis If Harry means that new cars cost too much for him to feel comfortable buying one, then this is a subjective claim. If Harry has in mind that the average cost of a new car is more than twice the federal government poverty standard for a family of four, then he would be using impersonal standards, and this is objective. Or Harry might have no standard in mind, in which case the sentence is too vague to be a claim.

If it is not clear what standard is being invoked, don't argue about the claim. The sentence is too vague.

Example 22 Markets are usually a good way to organize economic activity.

Analysis This is too vague to be a claim unless it's made clear what standard is being used for "good" and how often something has to happen for it to be "usually".

Example 23 "It is said that we 'need' more highways. Does this mean that we should have them regardless of the cost—that is, the value of forsaken alternatives? If someone says that 'we need' more teachers, does he mean that, if *he* had to pay the costs of getting more teachers, he would hire more? When someone says there is a 'need' for something, he should always be asked, 'In order to achieve what, at what cost of other goods or 'needs,' and at whose cost?' "

Analysis The authors here are making it clear how unclear standards can infect reasoning.

Sometimes people trade on vagueness to convince us that there is no standard. The defense attorney in trial of the policemen charged with beating Rodney King argued roughly:

If a suspect who is totally uncooperative is hit once by a policeman, then that's not unnecessary force. Nor twice, if he's resisting. Possibly three times. If he's still resisting, shouldn't the policeman have the right to hit him again? It would be dangerous not to allow that. That means you can't tell me exactly how many times a policeman has to hit a suspect before it's unnecessary force. So the policeman did not use unnecessary force.

He was saying that if you can't make the difference precise, there is no difference. But in general that's wrong: In an auditorium lit by a single candle there are some parts that are clearly lit and some parts that are clearly dark, even if we can't draw a precise line where it stops being light and begins being dark.

> **Drawing the line fallacy** It's bad reasoning when someone argues that if you can't make the difference precise, then there is no difference.

Sentences that appear to state a moral position are not easy to classify or debate. If they're meant as objective, then the impersonal standards that are being invoked must be made clear.

Example 24 Capitalism is evil.

Analysis If you hear someone say this, you can bet they mean it to be taken as objective. And given an objective standard of what is meant by "evil", it will be objective, regardless of how much disagreement there is about whether it's true or false.

Sometimes when you challenge people to make things clearer, they'll say, "I just mean it's wrong (right) to me." When you press them, though, it turns out they're not so happy when you disagree. They're just being defensive, and what they really mean is "I have a right to believe that." Of course they do. But do they have a good reason to believe it? It's rare that people intend moral views to be subjective.

1.2 Definitions

Definitions are one of the best ways to clarify our thinking.
In this section we'll see how to recognize, make, and use them.

> **Definition**   A definition is an explanation or stipulation of how to use a word or phrase.

A definition is not true or false, but good or bad, apt or wrong. Definitions tell us what we're talking about. Claims are what we use to make assertions about that subject.

A definition is not a claim.

Example 1 "Exogenous" means "developing from without".
   Analysis   This is a definition, not a claim. It is an explanation of how to use the word "exogenous".

Example 2 Puce is the color of a flea, purplish brown or brownish purple.
   Analysis   This is a definition, not a claim.

People often hide a claim that should be debated behind an apparent definition. A *persuasive definition* is not a definition but rather a claim that should be argued for masquerading as a definition.

Example 3 A capitalist is someone who thinks that money is more important than people.
   Analysis   This is a persuasive definition. What should be argued for, namely, whether capitalists think money is more important than people, is being assumed as an apparent definition.

Example 4 By bourgeoisie is meant the class of modern capitalists, owners of the means of social production and employers of wage-labour; by proletariat, the class of modern wage-labourers who, having no means of production of their own, are reduced to selling their labour power in order to live.
Marx and Engels, Manifesto of the Communist Party

   Analysis   In the apparent definition of "proletariat" the word "reduced" conceals the claim that the proletariat are exploited, which makes that a persuasive definition.

Economists often attach special meanings to common words by stipulating their meaning. We have to be careful to note their definitions.

Example 5 "*Resources* are factors of production classified as land, labor, and capital."
   Analysis   The author has clearly stipulated what this word will mean in his text, though that might not be how we usually understand "resources".

Example 6 Every man is rich or poor according to the degree in which he can afford to enjoy the necessaries, conveniences, and amusements of human life.   Adam Smith, *The Wealth of Nations*

Analysis Smith has made clear how he understands "rich", though you might not agree.

Example 7 It is of an Anarchist-Communist society we are about to speak, a society that recognizes the absolute liberty of the individual, that does not admit of any authority, and makes use of no compulsion to drive men to work.   Kropotkin, *The Conquest of Bread*

Analysis Not all definitions come with a sign that says "Here comes a definition." In this passage the definition is embedded in a longer sentence.

Example 8 "*Capital* is the physical plants, machinery, and equipment used to produce other goods. Capital goods are human-made goods that do not directly satisfy human wants."

Analysis The first sentence is a definition. If the second sentence is meant to clarify the definition, it appears wrong, while if it is meant as a claim about capital goods, it seems false: Capital goods do directly satisfy human wants, in particular the want of the capitalist to have a good piece of machinery and more profit. Assuming the author knows what he's talking about, we need a definition of "human wants" and "directly" to make sense of this passage.

Example 9 We, the Republican Party, as long as I am chairman, will run a positive campaign. All statements will be based on the truth and the records.

John Dendahl, Chairman of the Republican Party in New Mexico,
quoted in the *Albuquerque Tribune*

Analysis We have to take the term "positive campaign" to be defined in the context of this passage, since nowhere else in the interview does Dendahl define it. But it's a persuasive definition, since most of us think a positive campaign is one in which dirt is not thrown, even if the dirt is true.

These problems with definitions show that we need to be clear about what a good definition is.

> **Good definition**   A good definition satisfies the following criteria:
>
> • The words doing the defining are clear and better understood than the word or phrase being defined.
>
> • The words being defined and the defining phrase can be used interchangeably. That is, it's correct to use the one exactly when it's correct to use the other.
>
> A definition is **too broad** if it covers cases it shouldn't.
> A definition is **too narrow** if it misses cases it should cover.

Example 10 "*Equity* means that the benefits of those resources are distributed fairly among society's members."

Analysis This is a bad definition. The author needs to tell us what he means by the vague word "fairly": according to need? to productivity? equally? Some people think that "fairly" means "from each according to his ability to each according to his need."

Example 11   —Maria's so rich, she can afford to buy you dinner.
  —What do you mean by "rich"?
  —She's got a Mercedes.
  Analysis This is not a definition, or it's a very bad one. Some people who have a Mercedes aren't rich, so the definition is too broad; some people who are rich don't own one, so the definition is also too narrow. That Maria has a Mercedes might be evidence that she's rich.

Example 12 "This leaves close to a third of GDP for all *nonconsumption* uses. Government services take up 17 percent, buying such things as airplanes, guns, and the services of soldiers, teachers, and bureaucrats. The rest is mainly business purchases of machinery and industrial structures (about 12 percent of GDP) and consumer purchases of new houses (4 percent)."
  Analysis It may appear that the author is defining "nonconsumption uses" as government services, business purchases of machinery and industrial structures, and consumer purchases of new houses. But that's so far from our ordinary understanding of "nonconsumption", it's hard to be sure.

Example 13 "*Less-developed countries* The economies of Asia, Africa, and Latin America."
  Analysis This is a bad definition. A country is not an economy. Even viewing that as a typo, the definition would be too broad: Japan is in Asia, and no one classifies it as less-developed. The definition is also too narrow: Bulgaria is in Europe and is currently classified as less-developed.

Good definitions come from a process of reflection about what we mean when we use words or what we want to express with a single term. If you are aware of the steps needed in making a good definition, you should be better able to evaluate definitions you encounter.

Steps in making a good definition

1. Show the need for a definition.

2. State the definition.

3. Make sure the words make sense.

4. Give examples where the definition applies.

5. Give examples where the definition does not apply.

6. If necessary, contrast it with other likely definitions.

7. Possibly revise your definition.

The key to making a good definition is to look for examples where the definition does or does not apply to make sure that it is not too broad or too narrow. For example, suppose we want to define "school cafeteria". That's something a lawmaker might need in order to write a law to disburse funds for a food program. As a first go, we might try "A place in a school where students eat." But that's too broad, since that would include just a room where students can take their meals. So we could try "A place in a school where students can buy a meal." But that's too broad, too, since that could include a room where you could buy a sandwich from a vending machine. How about "A room in a school where students can buy a hot meal that is served on a tray"? But if there's a fast-food restaurant like Burger King at the school, that would qualify. So it looks like we need "A room in a school where students can buy a hot meal that is served on a tray, and the school is responsible for the preparation and selling of the food." This looks better, though if adopted as a definition in a law it might keep schools that want money from the legislature from contracting out the preparation of their food. Whether that's too narrow will depend on how the lawmakers intend the money to be spent.

Example 14 "In the broadest sense, production is the act of increasing one's utility. *Exchange* of existing goods is *productive* because, as we have seen, it increases one's utility. Production also can occur when the physical attributes of resources—including their time of availability, place, or form—are changed. We shall bow to convention and restrict the label 'production' to the changing or creating of goods and services—that is, wealth."

Analysis This is an example of a carefully made and explained definition.

Example 15 Taxes are either direct or indirect. A direct tax is one which is demanded from the very persons who, it is intended or desired, should pay it. Indirect taxes are those which are demanded from one person in the expectation and intention that he shall indemnify himself at the expense of another: such as the excise or customs. The producer or importer of a commodity is called upon to pay a tax on it, not with the intention to levy a peculiar contribution upon him, but to tax through him the consumers of the commodity, from whom it is supposed that he will recover the amount by means of an advance in price.   J. S. Mill, *Principles of Political Economy*

Analysis These are careful definitions with an explanation.

1.3 Concealed Claims

In this section we'll see how people can try to convince us by a choice of words rather than reasoning, concealing what they ought to be proving.

> **Slanter** A slanter is any choice of words that attempts to convince by concealing a dubious claim.

A persuasive definition, for example, is a slanter. Slanters are bad because they try to get us to assume a dubious claim is true without reflecting on it by concealing it from inspection.

Often people try to conceal a claim with a question that presupposes that it is true. The best response to a *loaded question* is to point out the concealed claim and begin discussing that.

Example 1 When are you planning to start studying in this course?
Analysis This is a loaded question, and the best response is to say, "What makes you think I'm not studying hard already?"

Example 2 When will the President do something to try to reduce inflation?
Analysis This is a loaded question.

Probably the most common way to slant an exposition is to use one of the following.

> **Euphemism** A euphemism is a word or phrase that makes something sound better than a neutral description.
> **Dysphemism** A dysphemism is a word or phrase that makes something sound worse than a neutral description.

Example 3 The United States should not give money to the Russian government because of its repression of the freedom fighters in Chechnya.
Analysis To call the guerrillas in Chechnya "freedom fighters" is to say that they are fighting to liberate their country and give their countrymen freedom. The Russian government calls those people "terrorists", which is to classify them as bad, inflicting violence for their own partisan political ends without popular support.

Related to dysphemisms are *downplayers*: a word or phrase that minimizes the significance of a claim. An *up-player* is a kind of euphemism using a word or phrase that exaggerates the significance of a claim.

10

Example 4 Zoe: Hey, Mom! Great news. I managed to pass my first econ exam.

Mom: You only just passed?

Analysis Zoe has up-played the significance of what she did, trying to convince her mother to believe "It took great effort to pass" with the word "managed". Her mother downplayed the significance of passing by using "only just" without saying the claim, "Passing but not getting a good grade is not commendable."

Other ways of downplaying are with "scare" quotes or with words that restrict or limit the meaning of others.

Example 5 "Economic liberals, on the other hand, are concerned about the effects of free trade on U.S. workers and businesses. They argue that government intervention in the form of quotas and tariffs is necessary to protect U.S. citizens from 'unfair' trade practices in foreign countries."

Analysis The scare quotes here conceal the claim that the trade practices aren't really unfair.

Example 6 Purchasing this newsletter and following our investing advice for the stock market will guarantee you a return of at least 9% per year.[1]

Analysis The footnote qualifies the guarantee, making it worthless. Do you think you'll be around in forty-seven years to hold this newsletter accountable, and will this newsletter even be in business to make good on the guarantee that far in the future?

Sometimes a claim is worded to weasel out of its apparent meaning.

Example 7 The Secretary of Health and Human Services announced today that she is very sorry people took her words to be racial slurs.

Analysis You can bet she's sorry that people took her words that way. But she certainly hasn't apologized.

A very common way to try to get people to accept what you say is to browbeat them into thinking you have a proof without ever giving one, that is, offering a ***proof substitute***.

Example 8 Dr. E: By now you must have been convinced what a great teacher I am. It's obvious to anyone. Of course, some people are a little slow. But surely you see it.

Analysis Dr. E didn't prove that he is a great teacher, though he made it sound as if he were proving something. He was just reiterating the claim, trying to intimidate his students into believing it with the words "obvious", "some people are a little slow", "surely", and "must have been convinced".

Example 9 Having regard to the excessive burden of many types of debt, it can only be an inexperienced person who would prefer the former.

Keynes, *The General Theory of Employment*

Analysis So you're just inexperienced if you disagree with Keynes.

Example 10 So much has already been written on currency that of those who give their attention to such subjects none but the prejudiced are ignorant of its true principles. I shall, therefore, take only a brief survey of some of the general laws which regulate its quantity and value.

Ricardo, *Principles of Political Economy*

Analysis And if you disagree with Ricardo you're prejudiced!

---

[1] Purchaser agrees to hold all investments for at least forty-seven years.

Example 11   Tillage, indeed, in that part of ancient Italy which lay in the neighbourhood of Rome, must have been very much discouraged by the distributions of corn which were frequently made to the people, either gratuitously, or at a very low price.   Adam Smith, *The Wealth of Nations*

Analysis   There's no argument here. Just a proof substitute, "must have been", for which we should read "I bet that it was." Social scientists sometimes use that phrase and others like "it is likely that" in place of serious argument.

Example 12   "For a dollar of current consumption sacrificed, more than a dollar of income is obtainable in the future. That *net* increase is called the *net marginal productivity of investment.* Plant a seed today and next year have more than one seed. The more we act according to this law of nature, the larger the *net* marginal productivity of investment."

Analysis   Saying that the claim "Plant a seed today and next year have more than one seed" is a "law of nature" is a proof substitute which the authors use to get you to accept their analysis: If it's a law of nature it's got to be true. But actually it's false, as we discovered when we planted an acre of grass seed and none of it germinated.

People also try to conceal that they have no support for their claim by trying to *shift the burden of proof.*

Example 13   Tom: America should adopt a strong currency policy.
Maria: Why?
Tom: Why not?
Analysis   Tom hasn't given any reason to think his claim is true. He's only invited Maria to say why she thinks it's false, so he can attack, which is easier than supporting a position.

You may be tempted to use slanters in your own writing. *Don't.* Slanters turn off those you want to convince. Worse, though they may work for the moment, they don't stick. Without reinforcement, the other person will remember only the joke or jibe. A good argument can last and last—the other person can see the point clearly and reconstruct it. Worse, if you use slanters, the other person can destroy your points not by facing your real argument, but by pointing out the slanters.

If you reason calmly and well, you will earn the respect of others
and may learn that others merit your respect, too.

Example 14   "Wages for the same kind of labor are lower in the South than in the North. Also, wages are lower in Puerto Rico than in the United States. How can a northern employee protect his wage level from the competition of lower-wage southern labor? And how can a laborer in the United States protect his job (and higher wage rate) from Puerto Rican labor? One device would be to advocate "equal pay for equal work" in the United States, including Puerto Rico, by legislating minimum wages higher than the prevailing level in the South and Puerto Rico. It should come as no surprise to learn that in the United States support for minimum-wage laws comes primarily from northerners who profess to be trying to help the poorer southern laborers."

Analysis   The word "profess" here conceals the claim that northern workers—on the whole—are duplicitous: those workers say they're trying to help their southern counterparts when they're really motivated by self-interest. But the authors have given no reason to believe that northern workers are not entirely sincere. Noticing how the authors have used a slanter here, we can be on the alert for this bias in their work.

2   Arguments

When we try to convince someone that a claim is true because it follows from some other claims, we are making an argument. We need to understand what an argument is, how to evaluate arguments, and how to interpret arguments before we can look at any other kinds of reasoning.

In Section 2.1 we clarify what an argument is and give the most basic standards for determining whether an argument is good or bad. Part of that is deciding whether the assumptions of the argument are true, which is what we consider in Section 2.2.

Most arguments we encounter, however, are not complete. But that needn't mean they are bad. We need standards for how to interpret arguments—how to repair them—in order to determine whether we should accept their conclusions. That's the work of Section 2.3.

2.1 Arguments

In this section we'll explain what an argument is and what standards we use to say whether an argument is good or bad.

Argument   An argument is an attempt to convince someone (possibly yourself) that a particular claim, called the **conclusion**, is true. The rest of the argument is a collection of claims called the **premises**, which are given as the reasons for believing the conclusion is true.

The conclusion is sometimes called the **issue** that is being debated.

Example 1   Economics is the most important subject in school. It will help you make better financial decisions, it will help you get a job, and it will help you understand political debates.

Analysis   This is an argument. The *conclusion* is "Economics is the most important subject in school." The *premises*, that is, the reasons given for why we should believe the conclusion, are "Economics will help you make better financial decisions," "Economics will help you get a job," "Economics will help you understand political debates."

Example 2   You can tell that economics graduates are smart. They get high-paying jobs, and they always dress well.

Analysis   This is an argument with the conclusion "Economics graduates are smart." The evidence (premises) given for that is "Economics graduates get high-paying jobs" and "Economics graduates dress well."

Example 3   Follow the directions for using this medicine provided by your doctor. This medicine may be taken on an empty stomach or with food. Store this medicine at room temperature, away from heat and light.

Analysis   This is not an argument. Instructions or commands are not an attempt to convince anyone that a claim is true.

Example 4   It is not from the benevolence of the butcher, the brewer, or the baker that we expect our dinner, but from their regard to their own interest. We address ourselves, not to their humanity but to their self-love, and never talk to them of our own necessities but of their advantages. Nobody but a beggar chooses to depend entirely upon the benevolence of his fellow-citizens. Even a beggar does not depend on it entirely. The charity of well-disposed people, indeed, supplies him with the whole fund of his subsistence. But though this principle ultimately provides him with all the necessaries of life which he has occasion for, it neither does nor can provide him with them as he has occasion for them. The greater part of his occasional wants are supplied in the same manner as those of other people, by treaty, by barter, and by purchase.   Adam Smith, *The Wealth of Nations*

Analysis   There's no argument here. Smith expands and illustrates his claim about people to make it seem more plausible, but he's not asking us to believe it because it follows from other claims.

14

Certain words can signal to us that a passage should be seen as an argument.

> **Indicator Word** A word or phrase added to a claim to tell us the role of the claim in an argument or what the speaker thinks of the claim or argument.

Conclusion indicators: hence; therefore; so; thus; consequently; we can then show that; it follows that; . . .

Premise indicators: since; because; for; in as much as; given that; suppose that; it follows from; on account of; due to; . . .

Indicators of speaker's belief: probably; certainly; most likely; I think; . . .

For an argument to be good, it must give good reason to believe its conclusion is true. But what do we mean by "good reason"?

If we don't have good reason to believe the premises, then they can't provide good reason to believe the conclusion. From a false premise we can derive both false conclusions and true conclusions, as the next two examples show.

Example 5 All Asian countries use the U.S. dollar as their currency. Japan is in Asia. So Japan uses the U.S. dollar as its currency.

Analysis This argument has a false premise and a false conclusion.

Example 6 All Asian countries use the U.S. dollar as their currency. Japan is in Asia. The U.S. dollar is convertible into all other currencies. So the currency of Japan is convertible into any other currency.

Analysis This argument has the same false premise, but a true conclusion.

> **Plausible claims** A claim is plausible if we have good reason to believe it is true. It is less plausible the less reason we have to believe it is true. It is *implausible* if we have no reason to believe it is true.

An argument can be no better than its least plausible premise. But plausible premises are not enough to guarantee that an argument is good. If the premises are no more plausible than the conclusion, then they give us no reason to believe the conclusion.

Example 7 Expanding the North American Free Trade Association to include Chile will raise the GNP of Chile by 5%. Therefore, NAFTA will be accepted by the Chilean government.

Analysis This is a bad argument: "Expanding the North American Free Trade Association to include Chile will raise the GNP of Chile by 5%" is no more plausible than "NAFTA will be accepted by the Chilean government."

> **Begging the question** An argument begs the question if one of its premises is no more plausible than its conclusion.

One more criterion is needed for an argument to be good: The premises must support the conclusion. That is, the conclusion must follow from the premises.

Example 8   You are reading this book. This book is about critical thinking. Therefore, this book is a paperback.
   Analysis   The premises and conclusion here are clearly true. But the premises don't support the conclusion. They give us no reason to believe the conclusion.

Example 9   Dollar bills are printed using green ink. Therefore, U.S. currency is easy to counterfeit.
   Analysis   Our reaction to the single true premise here should be "So?" Why does "U.S. currency is easy to counterfeit" follow from that?

Valid argument   An argument is valid if it is impossible for the premises to be true and the conclusion false (at the same time); otherwise it is invalid.

Strong and weak arguments   Invalid arguments are classified on a scale from strong to weak. An argument is strong if it's very unlikely for the premises to be true and the conclusion false (at the same time); an argument is weak if it is likely for the premises to be true and the conclusion false.

*The conclusion **follows from** the premises* means the argument is valid or strong.

Either an argument is valid or it isn't. But *the strength of an invalid argument is a matter of degree.*

   These definitions are the most important in the book. The diagram below should be very clear to you before you go any further. Refer to it often.

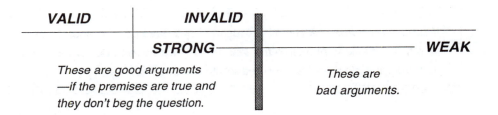

VALID	INVALID
	STRONG ——————————————————— WEAK
These are good arguments —if the premises are true and they don't beg the question.	These are bad arguments.

Example 10   All dogs bark. Ralph is a dog. Therefore, Ralph barks.
   Analysis   This is a valid argument. It is impossible for the premises to be true and the conclusion false at the same time.
   But the argument is bad. The first premise is false: Basenjis can't bark, some dogs have had their vocal cords cut, . . . Whether an argument is valid or strong depends on the relation between the premises and conclusion, not on whether the premises actually happen to be true. *Valid ≠ good.*

Example 11   All parakeets anyone I know has ever seen or heard or read about are under 2 feet tall. Therefore, the parakeets for sale at the mall are under 2 feet tall.
   Analysis   This is a strong argument. Surveying all the ways the premise could be true, we think that yes, a new supergrow bird food could have been formulated and the parakeets at the local mall are really 3 feet tall, we just haven't heard about it. Or a rare giant parakeet from the Amazon

forest could have been discovered and brought here. Or a UFO might have abducted a parakeet, hit it with growing rays, and the bird is gigantic. So the argument is not valid. But all these ways the premise could be true and the conclusion false are so unlikely that we have very good reason to believe the conclusion if the premise is true—though the conclusion still might be false.

Example 12   Good teachers give fair exams. Dr. E gives fair exams. So Dr. E is a good teacher.

Analysis   This is a weak argument. Dr. E might bore his students to tears and just copy good exams from the instructor's manual. Or he might get good exams from another teacher. There are lots of possibilities that are not unlikely.

Why should we worry whether the conclusion follows from the premises if we don't know that the premises are true? Consider what happens when a couple applies for a home loan. They fill out all the forms and give them to the loan officer at the bank. She reads their answers. At that point she might tell them that they don't qualify: Even though she doesn't know if the claims they made about their income and assets are true, she can see that even if they are true, they won't qualify for a loan. On the other hand, she might tell them that they'll qualify—if those claims are true. Then she'll have to make phone calls, check credit references, and so on, to find out if what they claimed is true. It's the same with arguments: Sometimes it's easier to evaluate first whether an argument is valid or strong in order to find out whether we should bother to investigate whether the premises are true.

How do we show that an argument is *not* valid or strong? We give an example, some *way* the world might be in which the premises would be true and the conclusion false.

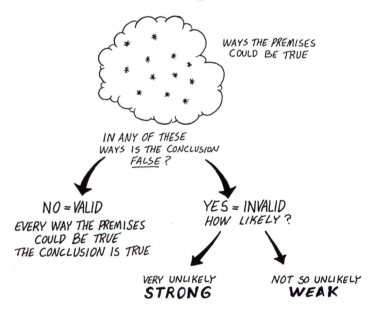

To reason well you must use your imagination.

Now we can summarize the conditions we need for an argument to be good.

> **Tests for an argument to be good**
> - The premises are plausible.
> - The premises are more plausible than the conclusion.
> - The argument is valid or strong.

Before you proceed any further in this text, you should be very clear that:

- Every good argument is valid or strong.
- Not every valid or strong argument is good (it could have a dubious premise).
- Only invalid arguments are classified from strong to weak.
- Every weak argument is bad.
- If the conclusion of a valid argument is false, one of the premises must be false.

Here are some examples to reinforce these points.

Example 13   Señora Vez is an economics professor. All economics professors are socialists. So Señora Vez is a socialist.
    Analysis   This is a valid argument: It is impossible for the premises to be true and the conclusion false. But it's a bad argument because the second premise is false.

Example 14   Dick is a bachelor. So Dick was never married.
    Analysis   This is weak. There is a not unlikely way that the premise could be true and the conclusion false: Dick could be divorced.

Example 15   Sandra's hair is naturally brown. Today Sandra's hair is red. So Sandra dyed her hair.
    Analysis   Sandra might be taking a new medication that has a strong effect. Or she might have been too close to her car when they were painting it, or . . . These are ways the premises could be true and the conclusion false, so the argument is not valid. But these are very unlikely, so the argument is strong. If the premises are true, it's good.

Example 16   The Standard and Poor's index rose 4% today. Dick has $2,000 in an S&P index mutual fund. So Dick's mutual fund account went up $80 today.
    Analysis   This is a valid argument: It's impossible for its premises to be true and the conclusion false. Whether it is good depends on whether its premises are true.

Example 17   Whenever Spot barks, there's a cat outside. Since he's barking now, there must be a cat outside.
    Analysis   This is a valid argument: There is no way the premise could be true and the conclusion false. But it's a bad argument: Perhaps Spot is barking at the garbageman. That possibility doesn't show the argument is weak—it shows that the first premise is false.

Example 18   All the dockworkers at Boa Vista docks belong to the union. Ralph has been working at the Boa Vista docks for two years. So probably Ralph belongs to the union, too.
    Analysis   "Probably" is an indicator word about the speaker's belief; the conclusion here is "Ralph belongs to the union." The argument is valid, *regardless of what the speaker thought.*

2.2 Evaluating Premises

In this section we develop a guide for deciding when to believe
an unsupported claim, which we need in evaluating the premises
of an argument.

We want criteria for when to believe an unsupported claim. But we have to be clear
that when we don't have good reason to believe a claim, that does not mean we have reason
to believe it's false. We might have no evidence that it's true or that it's false, in which case
we should suspend judgment.

not believe ≠ believe is false

lack of evidence ≠ evidence it is false

Three attitudes we can take to the truth of a claim

- Accept the claim as true.

- Reject the claim as false.

- Suspend judgment.

Example 1 Your school will raise tuition 12% next year.
  Analysis If you don't know anything about this, suspend judgment.

We'll now present some criteria we can use to decide when to accept or reject an
unsupported claim. We give them in their order of importance.

Our most reliable source of information about the world is our own experience.

If you don't trust your own experience, whose experience do you trust? Do you
believe your boss when she says you didn't hurt your back when you lifted that crate?
The company doctor when he tells you that your back doesn't really hurt? As Groucho
Marx said, "Who are you going to believe, me or your own eyes?"

Still, there are times we shouldn't trust our experience, in particular when either:

- We have good reason to doubt our memory or our perceptions.

- The claim contradicts other experiences of ours and there is a good argument
  (theory) against the claim.

Example 2   I'm sure I told you to come here on Tuesday.

   Analysis   Be cautious about arguing with the washing-machine repairman if you had a bad head cold the day you arranged for him to make his service call.

Example 3   The world is flat.

   Analysis   Our untutored experience makes it seem that this is true. Nonetheless, we reject it because of other claims we've learned are true.

Sometimes a claim seems to be about our own experience, but it's really a conclusion drawn from our experience. For example, when Suzy met two Chinese students last week who are good at math, she concluded "All Chinese students are good at math," but all she was entitled to from her own experience is "Two Chinese students are good at math."

   In science, claims offered as personal experience are called ***observational claims***; when used as premises of an argument they're called the ***evidence*** for the conclusion. To avoid subjectivity, scientists prefer *reproducible* observations, ones that anyone can test.

> We can accept claims made by someone we know and trust who is an authority about that kind of claim.

For example, Zoe tells Harry to stay away from the area of town around S. 3rd. She's seen people doing drugs there and knows two people who have been held up in that neighborhood. Zoe is reliable, and her knowledge would matter about these claims.

   On the other hand, Tom's mother tells him he should major in economics so he can get ahead in life. Should he believe her? She can tell him about her friends' children. But what really are the chances of getting a good job with a degree in economics? It would be better to check at the local colleges where they keep records on hiring graduates. He shouldn't reject her claim; he should suspend judgment until he gets more information.

> We can accept claims that are made by a reputable authority whom we can trust as an expert on this kind of claim and who has no motive to mislead.

Example 4   Compare:
   (a) The Surgeon General announces that smoking is bad for your health.
   (b) The doctor hired by the tobacco company says there's no proof that smoking is addictive or causes lung cancer.
   (c) The new Surgeon General says that marijuana should be legal.

   Analysis   The Surgeon General is a reputable physician with expertise in epidemiology. Further, she's in a position to survey the research on the subject. We have no reason to suspect her motives. So it's reasonable to believe her.

   But is the doctor hired by the tobacco company an expert on smoking-related diseases, or an allergist, or a pediatrician, or . . . ? It matters for whether to trust his ability to interpret the data. And he has a motive to mislead. There's no reason to accept his claim.

   Nor is there any reason to accept the Surgeon General's pronouncements about what should be law. Though she's an authority figure, she's not an expert on law and society.

> We can accept a claim put forward in a reputable journal or reference source.

The New England Journal of Medicine, for example, is regularly quoted, and for good reason. The articles in it are subjected to *peer review*: Experts in the subject are asked to evaluate whether the research was done to the standards of their discipline. *The National Geographic* has less reliable standards, since they pay for their own research in order to sell their magazine. But it's pretty reliable about natural history and ethnography. What about *The Economist*? Are the articles in it peer-reviewed research or opinion pieces? And anyone can incorporate as the "American Institute for Economic Analysis" or any other title you like. If you don't know the source, there's no reason to accept its claims.

> We can accept a claim from a media source that is usually reliable and has no obvious motive to mislead, if the person being quoted is named.

It's up to you to decide from experience whether a source is usually reliable. Don't trust a news report that makes that decision for you by quoting unnamed "usually reliable sources". *There's never good reason to accept a claim in the media from an unnamed source.* Look also for possible bias in a media source because of its advertisers. Ask yourself, "Who will benefit from my believing this?"

There are no absolute rules for when to accept, reject, or suspend judgment about a claim. It's a skill, weighing up the following criteria, listed in order of importance.

Criteria for judging unsupported claims

Accept The claim is known by personal experience.
(Exceptions: Our memory is not good; there's a good argument against our understanding of our experience; it's not our experience at all, but what we've concluded from it.)

Reject The claim contradicts personal experience.

Reject The claim contradicts other claims we know to be true.

Accept The claim is made by someone we know and trust and who is an authority about that kind of claim.

Accept The claim is offered by a reputable authority whom we can trust as an expert about this kind of claim and who has no motive to mislead.

Accept The claim is put forward in a reputable journal or reference source.

Accept The claim is in a media source that's been reliable and has no obvious motive to mislead, if the source is named.

We don't have criteria for when to *suspend judgment* on a claim. That's the default attitude we should adopt whenever we don't have good reason to accept or to reject a claim.

Common mistakes in evaluating unsupported claims

A. *Arguing backwards*

Arguing backwards is to reason that because we have an argument with a true conclusion, its premises must be true. An argument is supposed to convince us that its conclusion is true, not that its premises are true.

Example 5   Your friend says, "All CEOs of computer software companies are rich. Bill Gates is a CEO of a computer software company. So Bill Gates is rich." Since you know that Bill Gates is rich, you decide the argument is good and that all CEOs of computer software companies are rich.

     Analysis   This is arguing backwards. There are lots of CEOs of small software companies that are struggling to make a living. An argument is supposed to convince us that its conclusion is true, not that its premises are true.

B. *Appeal to authority*

We saw above that we can often accept a claim based on authority. But it is a bad appeal to authority to say that we should accept a claim because a particular person said it when that person is not really an authority on the subject or has motive to mislead.

Example 6   —What do you think of the new tax plan the President announced?
     —It must be good, 'cause Dan Rather said so.
     Analysis   Not everything that Dan Rather says is true.

Example 7   Legalizing marijuana is a terrible idea, because my mom said so.
     Analysis   You should love your mother, not believe everything she says.

C. *Mistaking the person for the claim*

You're mistaking the person (or group) for the claim if you believe that the claim is false because of who said it. It's often right to suspend judgment on a claim if you don't consider the person who's making the claim to be a reputable authority on the subject. But saying that the claim is actually false because of who said it is a mistake in reasoning.

Example 8   I don't believe the tax cut will benefit the poorest in our society. That's just another lie our senator said.
     Analysis   This is mistaking the person for the claim. Politicians don't lie *all* the time. There's no shortcut for reading and reasoning about a claim in evaluating whether to accept it.

Example 9   There's no water shortage here in New Mexico. That's just one of those things the environmentalists say.
     Analysis   This is mistaking the group for the claim.

D. *Appeal to common belief*

An appeal to common belief is to accept a claim as true because a lot of other people believe it. Typically, such reasoning is a bad appeal to authority. For example:

> Everyone I know says that Consolidated Computers is a great investment.
> So I'm going to buy 500 shares—they can't all be wrong.

However, as with all these common mistakes, an appeal to common belief can be good if we have further evidence for the claim.

Example 10   You go to England and find that everyone there is driving on the left-hand side of the road. You conclude that you should, too.

   Analysis   This is a good reasoning, since you also know that every country allows driving on just one side.

Similar common mistakes in evaluating an argument

E. Mistaking the person for the argument

You're mistaking the person (or group) for the argument when you reject an argument as bad just because of who said it.

Example 11   —I listened to Ted Kennedy explaining why President Bush's tax plan won't help stimulate the economy.
   —Are you kidding? He's really left-wing, and besides, he killed someone while driving drunk.

   Analysis   This is mistaking the person for the argument. Kennedy's argument may be good even if you doubt Kennedy's qualifications to make the argument.

F. Phony refutation

To *refute* an argument is to show that it is bad. Often we think we can refute an argument by showing that the person who made it doesn't believe one of the premises or even the conclusion itself. But that's a phony refutation: Sincerity is not one of the criteria for an argument to be good.

Example 12   Harry: We should stop logging old-growth forests. There are very few of them left in the U.S. They are important watersheds and preserve wildlife. Once cut, we cannot recreate them.

   Tom: You say we should stop logging old-growth forests? Who are you kidding? You just built a log cabin on the mountain.

   Analysis   Tom's rejection of Harry's argument seems reasonable: Harry's actions betray the conclusion he's arguing for. But whether they do or not (perhaps the logs came from the land Harry's family cleared in a new-growth forest), Tom has not answered Harry's argument. Tom is not justified in ignoring an argument because of Harry's actions.

   If Harry were to respond to Tom by saying that the logs for his home weren't cut from an old-growth forest, he's been suckered. Tom got him to change the subject, and they will be deliberating an entirely different claim than he intended. It's a phony refutation.

> ***Whether a claim is true or false is not determined by who said it.***
>
> ***Whether an argument is good or bad is not determined by who made it.***

Above all, remember that personal experience is your best guide. Don't trust others more than yourself about what you know best. That's the mistake Suzy made here:

Suzy: Professor Zzzyzzx is going to be late for class today. I just saw him at the Buckhorn reading the newspaper and drinking a beer, and it's already 1:58.

Maria: What? Are you crazy? He's always on time.

Suzy: I guess you're right—he'll be on time.

2.3 Repairing Arguments

Many arguments we encounter are not formulated well enough to pass our tests. But they aren't really bad. In this section we'll formulate criteria for how to interpret arguments without putting words in other people's mouths.

Here is an example of an argument you might hear.

Suzy: I heard that Wanda has a pet.

Tom: It must be a dog, because I heard barking in her house yesterday. And I know she doesn't let people bring their pets over to her home.

It's missing a premise to be a good argument: "Almost any pet that barks is a dog." But why bother saying that? Everyone knows it. The argument is good enough without it.

But how are we justified in saying that the argument is good enough without that premise? In order to develop criteria for how to repair arguments, we first need to make some assumptions about the people with whom we reason.

The principle of rational discussion   We assume that the other person who is discussing with us or whose arguments we are evaluating:

1. Knows about the subject under discussion.

2. Is able and willing to reason well.

3. Is not lying.

Economists use the word "rational" differently, as we'll see in Section 5.3.

Not everyone always fits the criteria for rational discussion, so what good is this assumption? If not, then there's no point in reasoning with him or her.

- If he doesn't know about the subject, educate, don't debate.

- If he isn't able to reason well, teach him.

- If he isn't willing to reason well, walk away.

- If he's lying, then the only point of reasoning with him is to catch him in his lies.

Above all, it's not worthwhile reasoning with someone if he or she is irrational.

The mark of irrationality   A person is *irrational* if he or she recognizes that an argument is good but doesn't accept the conclusion.

What if you hear one argument for a claim and another argument against it, and you can't find a flaw in either? You should *suspend judgment* on which conclusion is true until you can investigate more.

Still, many people don't care if your argument is good. Why not use bad methods of persuasion? Why should you follow these rules and assume them of others? If you don't:

- You are denying the essentials of democracy.

- You are likely to degrade your own ability to evaluate arguments.

- You are not as likely to convince others.

If you once forfeit the confidence of your fellow citizens, you can never regain their respect and esteem. It is true that you may fool all the people some of the time; you can even fool some of the people all the time; but you can't fool all of the people all the time.   Abraham Lincoln

With the Principle of Rational Discussion, we can formulate a guide to help us evaluate arguments. Since the person is supposed to be able to reason well, we can add a premise to his or her argument only if it makes the argument stronger or valid and doesn't beg the question. Since the person isn't lying and knows the subject under discussion, any premise we add should be plausible, and plausible to that person. We can also delete a premise if that doesn't make the argument any worse.

Guide to repairing arguments   Given an (implicit) argument that is apparently defective, we are justified in *adding* a premise or conclusion if it satisfies the following three conditions:

1. The argument becomes stronger or valid.
2. The premise is plausible and would seem plausible to the other person.
3. The premise is more plausible than the conclusion.

If the argument is then valid or strong yet one of the original premises is false or dubious, we may *delete* that premise if the argument remains valid or strong.

We say a premise is ***irrelevant*** if we can delete it and the argument isn't any weaker.

We don't need to know what the speaker was thinking in order to find a claim that makes an argument strong or valid, so we take (1) to have priority over (2). By first trying to make the argument valid or strong, we show the other person what he or she needs to assume to make the argument good.

Sometimes, though, it's clear that an argument is bad and there's no point in trying to repair it. Here are criteria for when we can write off an argument as irreparably bad.

> ***Unrepairable arguments*** We can't repair an argument if:
>
> - There's no argument there.
> - The argument is so lacking in coherence that there's nothing obvious to add.
> - A premise it uses is false or dubious and cannot be deleted.
> - Two of its premises are contradictory, though you don't know which is false.
> - The obvious premise to add would make the argument weak.
> - The obvious premise to add to make the argument strong or valid is false.
> - The conclusion is clearly false.

The best way to learn how to use these new tools is to work through examples. Try evaluating the passages below before you read the analyses. Each is designed to highlight one of the points in the Guide to Repairing Arguments or in Unrepairable Arguments.

Example 1 No dog meows. So Spot does not meow.
   Analysis "Spot is a dog" is the only premise that will make this a valid or strong argument. So we add that. Then, if it's true, the argument is good. We don't add "Spot barks." That's true and may seem obvious to the person who stated the argument, but it doesn't make the argument any better. So adding it violates (1) of the Guide. *We repair only as needed.*

Example 2 All MBAs have at least five years of post-secondary education. So Lisa is an MBA.
   Analysis The obvious premise to add is "Lisa has at least five years of secondary education." But then the argument is still weak (Lisa could be a physician, or a mathematician, or . . .). *If the obvious premise to add makes the argument weak, the argument is unrepairable.*

Example 3 Dr. E is a good teacher because he gives fair exams.
   Analysis The unstated premise needed here is "Almost any teacher who gives fair exams is a good teacher." That gives a strong argument. But the claim is dubious, since a bad teacher could copy fair exams from the instructor's manual. (If you thought the claim that's needed is "Good teachers give fair exams," read Example 12 on p. 17 again.) *The argument can't be repaired because the obvious premise to add to make the argument strong or valid is false or dubious.*
   But can't we make it strong by adding, say, "Dr. E gives great explanations," "Dr. E never misses class," . . . ? Those may be true and perhaps obvious to the person. But adding them doesn't *repair* this argument—it makes a whole new argument. *Don't put words in someone's mouth.*

Example 4 You can tell that economics graduates are smart. They get high-paying jobs, and they always dress well.
   Analysis The argument is weak—and it *is* an argument: The last sentence is meant as evidence. But there's no obvious way to repair it, since it's false that anyone who gets a high-paying job and dresses well is smart. *The person apparently can't reason.*

Example 5 If you bought $1000 worth of Nortel stock one year ago, it would now be worth $49. If you bought $1000 worth of Budweiser—the beer, not the stock—one year ago, drank all the beer, and traded in the cans for the nickel deposit, you would have $79. So you should start drinking heavily and recycle if you want to stay ahead of the stock market.

Analysis   The conclusion is clearly false, so we don't need to try to figure out what's wrong with this argument. It's unrepairable.

Example 6   You shouldn't eat the fat on your steak. Haven't you heard cholesterol is bad for you?

Analysis   The conclusion is the first sentence. But what are the premises? The speaker's question is rhetorical, meant to be taken as an assertion: "Cholesterol is bad for you." But that alone won't give us the conclusion. We need something like "Steak fat has a lot of cholesterol" and "You shouldn't eat anything that's bad for you." *Premises like these are obvious to most people*, so we don't bother to say them. This argument is O.K.

Example 7   You're going to vote for the Green Party candidate for President? Don't you realize that means your vote will be wasted?

Analysis   Here, too, the questions are rhetorical, meant to be taken as assertions: "Don't vote for the Green Party candidate" (the conclusion) and "Your vote will be wasted" (the premise). This sounds reasonable, though something is missing. A visitor from Germany may not know "The Green Party candidate doesn't have a chance of winning." But she may also question why that matters. We'd have to fill in the argument further: "If you vote for someone who doesn't have a chance of winning, then your vote will be wasted." And when we add that premise we see the argument that used such "obvious" premises is really not good. Why should we believe that if you vote for someone who doesn't stand a chance of winning, then your vote is wasted? If that were true, then who wins is the only important result of an election, rather than, say, making a position understood by the electorate. At best we can say that when the unstated premises are added, we get an argument one of whose premises needs a substantial argument to convince us that it is true. *Using the Guide to Repairing Arguments can lead us to unstated assumptions about which the real debate should be.*

Example 8   Cats are more likely than dogs to carry diseases harmful to humans. Cats kill songbirds. Cats disturb people at night with their screeching and clattering in garbage cans. Cats leave pawprints on cars and will sleep in unattended cars. Cats are not as pleasant as dogs and are owned only by people who have satanic affinities. So there should be a leash law for cats just as much as for dogs.

Analysis   This letter to the editor is going pretty well until the next to last sentence. *That claim is a bit dubious and the argument would be just as strong without it. So we should delete it.* Then we have an argument which, with some unstated premises you can supply, is good.

Example 9   In a famous speech, Martin Luther King, Jr. said:

> I have a dream that one day this nation will rise up and live out the true meaning of its creed: "We hold these truths to be self-evident—that all men are created equal."
> . . . I have a dream that one day even the state of Mississippi, a desert state sweltering with the heat of injustice and oppression, will be transformed into an oasis of freedom and justice. I have a dream that my four little children will one day live in a nation where they will not be judged by the color of their skin but by the content of their character.

. . . King is also presenting a logical argument . . . the argument might be stated as follows; "America was founded on the principle that all men are created equal. This implies that people should not be judged by skin color, which is an accident of birth, but rather by what they make of themselves ('the content of their character'). To be consistent with this principle, America should treat black people and white people alike."

The Art of Reasoning, David Kelley

Analysis   The rewriting of this passage is too much of a stretch—putting words in someone's mouth—to be appropriate. Where did David Kelley get the premise "This implies . . ."? Stating your dreams and hoping others will share them is not an argument. Martin Luther King, Jr. knew how to argue well and could do so when he wanted. We're not going to make his speech more respectable by pretending it's an argument. *Not every good attempt to persuade is an argument.*

Example 10   Environmentalists should not be allowed to tell us what to do. The federal government should not be allowed to tell us what to do. Therefore, we should go ahead and allow logging in old-growth forests.

   Analysis   The speaker has confused whether we have the right to cut down forests with whether we should cut them down. The argument is weak; indeed, we could delete either premise and it wouldn't be any weaker. *The speaker's assumptions are irrelevant to the conclusion.*

Example 11   "And the problem of scarcity is real. Worldwide, some 15 children die every minute from lack of adequate nutrition and health care. The world's citizens lack basic education, shelter, clothing, clean water, and hygiene as well. Many of the world's nations lack basic infrastructure in the form of communications, transportation, sanitation, and electricity. Even in a prosperous country such as ours, some 12% of the population is poor. As we shall see in Chapter Seven on poverty, these people receive inadequate food, shelter, health care, clothing, and other necessities. Our nation as a whole lacks sufficient environmental protection, first-rate educational opportunities, and quality health care for all. Choices as to what we produce and how much we produce can easily become matters of life and death to some of our citizens."

   Analysis   This passage seems to be an argument, but what is its conclusion? If we take it to be trying to establish the first sentence, that the problem of scarcity is real, it is weak: All the problems listed could all be due to bad distribution rather than scarcity. But if we take the last sentence to be the conclusion, then it's a good argument. *Since we assume the author can reason well, we take the final sentence as conclusion.* Knowing how to repair arguments will make it easier to read your texts.

Example 12   "U.S. citizens are independent souls, and they tend to dislike being forced to do anything. The compulsory nature of Social Security therefore has been controversial since the program's beginnings. Many conservatives argue that Social Security should be made voluntary, rather than compulsory."

   Analysis   The first two sentences look like an argument. But the first sentence is too vague to be a claim. So *we can't view this as an argument*, and hence there's certainly no repair for it.

Example 13   The bourgeoisie, wherever it has got the upper hand, has put an end to all feudal, patriarchal, idyllic relations. It has pitilessly torn asunder the motley feudal ties that bound man to his "natural superiors," and has left no other bond between man and man than naked self-interest, than callous "cash payment."   Marx and Engels, *Manifesto of the Communist Party*

   Analysis   Marx and Engels use words you might not be familiar with, but that's no reason to dismiss this passage. *A dictionary is an important tool in critical thinking.* Once you understand all the words, you'll see that this passage is not an argument. Either you accept what Marx and Engels are saying, or you don't. They haven't given any reason to believe their claims.

Example 14   In any particular future year, whatever the "retirement security" system in place, the U.S. can consume only what it produces. So the national standard of living depends entirely on the productivity of the working population. The only way to make up for a larger number of dependents per worker is higher productivity, and the route to higher productivity in the future is more saving and investment, more technological progress, and more education and training now.
                              Robert M. Solow, "The Party Line", *New York Review of Books*, April 11, 2002
   Analysis   This passage has one argument:

The U.S. can consume only what it produces.
So the national standard of living depends entirely on the productivity
of the working population.

Relative to the usual understanding of "national standard of living", this is a valid argument. But the premise is false: Forcing other countries to give or sell goods, such as oil, at lower prices can increase what the U.S. consumes. So it's unrepairable—unless, perhaps, Solow has a different notion of the productivity of a country, counting war or intimidation as a mode of production. *Looking for what is needed to make an argument good can lead us to find crucial unstated assumptions that should be debated.*

Example 15 [The distribution of wealth] is a matter of human institution solely. The things once there, mankind, individually or collectively, can do with them as they like. They can place them at the disposal of whomsoever they please, and on whatever terms. Further, in the social state, in every state except total solitude, any disposal whatever of them can only take place by the consent of society, or rather of those who dispose of its active force. Even what a person has produced by his individual toil, unaided by any one, he cannot keep, unless by the permission of society. Not only can society take it from him, but individuals could and would take it from him, if society only remained passive; if it did not either interfere *en masse*, or employ and pay people for the purpose of preventing him from being disturbed in the possession. The distribution of wealth, therefore, depends on the laws and customs of society. The rules by which it is determined, are what the opinions and feelings of the ruling portion of the community make them, and are very different in different ages and countries; and might be still more different, if mankind so chose.
John Stuart Mill, *Principles of Political Economy*

Analysis This is a long passage, but it's worth struggling through. Mill gives a good argument, and he lays it out well. He *announces his conclusion at the start*. He then establishes it and more clearly restates it after "therefore". He then explains what that means.

Example 16 It is only for the sake of profit that any man employs capital in the support of industry; and he will always, therefore, endeavour to employ it in the support of that industry of which the produce is likely to be of greatest value, or to exchange for the greatest quantity either of money or of other goods.
Adam Smith, *The Wealth of Nations*

Analysis The argument is valid, but *its single premise is false*: Lots of other considerations about where to invest their capital matter to many people: convenience, social responsibility, ... So there's no way to repair it, and it's bad.

Example 17 (1) Investors in 1997 invested more than twice as much money in no-load mutual funds as in other mutual funds. So, (2) Investors in 1997 overwhelmingly preferred no-load mutual funds.

Analysis In Section 1.1 we said that (2) is subjective and (1) is objective. Typically, we invoke some evidence such as (1) to conclude (2). But to have a good argument for (2) we also need a premise like "When someone invests money in a fund, they prefer that fund to one that they do not invest in", which is plausible and makes this a good argument. That subjective claim is the link between the observed behavior and the inferred state of mind. Often *an unstated assumption linking behavior to thoughts is needed to make an argument good.*

Example 18 "The winners from international trade gain more than the losers lose; U.S. sellers gain more from international trade than U.S. buyers lose, and foreign sellers gain more than foreign buyers lose. As a result, international trade is economically efficient."

Analysis This is an argument. The premise is "The winners from international trade gain more than the losers lose." The conclusion is "International trade is economically efficient." With the understanding economists give to the words "economically efficient", this is a valid argument. Whether it is good depends on whether the premise is true. It might seem that the rest of the first sentence establishes that premise, but really it's only repeating the premise in different words.

When someone leaves a conclusion unsaid, he or she is ***implying*** the conclusion. When you decide that an unstated claim is either an unstated conclusion or is needed to make an argument good, you are ***inferring*** that claim. More generally, we say that someone is implying a claim if in context it's clear that he or she believes the claim, and in that case we say that we are inferring the claim.

Example 19 I'm not going to vote, because no matter who is mayor, nothing is going to get done to repair the roads in this part of town.

Analysis An unstated claim is needed to make sense of what is said: "If no matter who is mayor nothing is going to get done to repair the roads in this part of town, then you shouldn't vote for mayor." We infer this from the person's remarks; he or she has implied it.

Example 20 Supervisor: My best workers never take a break.

Analysis You might think Tom's supervisor is implying that he should never take a break if he wants her to consider him one of her best workers. But she could say he inferred incorrectly: She was just making an observation.

3 Reasoning with Special Kinds of Claims

Certain kinds of claims require special skills to analyze.

In Section 3.1 we look at claims made from other claims using the words "or" and "not". Then we consider how to reason with compound claims that use "if . . . then . . .". Those are essential for reasoning about hypothetical situations. We'll learn how to recognize specific kinds of arguments as valid or weak by inspecting their form with respect to those words. We'll also see how to form the contradictory of a claim and how to analyze claims that talk about necessary and sufficient conditions.

With that as background, we can learn how to refute an argument or claim in Section 3.2.

In Section 3.3 we look at claims about some portion of a collection, whether all, or some, almost all, or a very few. These general claims are what we use when we want to quantify in a very general manner, and we need to be aware of typical mistakes and typical good arguments that use those.

Of special importance in economics and in our daily lives are normative claims, claims that state what we think should or should not be done, based on some value judgment. We'll study those in Section 3.4.

3.1 Compound Claims

We can combine claims using the words "or", "not", and "if . . . then . . .". In this section we'll learn how to form contradictories of such claims and how to analyze talk of necessary and sufficient conditions. We'll see also that certain arguments that use such claims can be recognized as valid or weak solely by their form.

> **Compound claim** A compound claim is one that is composed of other claims but has to be viewed as just one claim.

Example 1 Either the Federal Reserve Board will raise interest rates or there will be inflation.
 Analysis This is a compound claim composed of the claims "The Federal Reserve Board will raise interest rates" and "There will be inflation", joined by the word "or". Whether it is true or false depends on whether one or both of its parts are true.

> **Alternatives** In a compound "or" claim, the parts are the alternatives.

Example 2 Either a Democrat or a Republican will win the election.
 Analysis We can view this as an "or" claim with alternatives: "A Democrat will win the election" and "A Republican will win the election."

Example 3 The Green Party candidate will not win the election.
 Analysis This is a compound claim derived from "The Green Party candidate will win the election" by adding the word "not".

Example 4 There will be inflation because the President will declare war.
 Analysis This is not a compound claim. It's an argument: "because" is an indicator word.

Essential to reasoning well is knowing how to disagree, how to assert the opposite of what someone else has said.

> **Contradictory of a claim** A contradictory of a claim is a claim that must have the opposite truth-value.

Example 5 Spot is barking.
 Analysis A contradictory is "Spot is not barking."

Example 6 Inflation will be less than 3% this year.

32

Analysis   We can contradict this by saying, "Inflation will not be less than 3% this year." But we can also contradict the example by saying, "Inflation will be 3% or more this year", which doesn't have the word "not" in it.

In order to discuss the form of claims and some valid forms of arguments that use compound claims, we'll use the following conventions in the discussions and diagrams:

The letters A and B stand for any claims.

An arrow (———►) stands for "therefore".

We write "not A" to stand for any contradictory of A.

The symbol "+" means an additional premise.

> **Contradictory of an "or" claim**   A *or* B has contradictory *not* A *and not* B.
>
> **Contradictory of an "and" claim**   A *and* B has contradictory *not* A *or not* B.

Example 7   Suzy will invest in bonds or she will invest in gold.
   Contradictory   Suzy won't invest in bonds and she won't invest in gold.

Example 8   The President or the Secretary of State will visit Israel this month.
   Contradictory   Neither the President nor the Secretary of State will visit Israel this month. Another contradictory of "A or B" is *neither* A *nor* B.

Here is the first example of a kind of argument whose validity we can recognize just by considering its form:

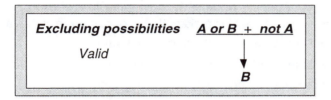

> **Excluding possibilities**   **A or B + not A**
>
> *Valid*
>
> **B**

Example 9   Either the Federal Reserve Bank will raise interest rates or unemployment will fall below 4%. The Federal Reserve Bank will not raise interest rates. So unemployment will fall below 4%.
   Analysis   This is a valid argument of the form "excluding possibilities".

We could reason equally well with more than two alternatives: "A or B or C; not A; not B; therefore C" is valid, too. Or we can exclude just some of the possibilities.

Example 10   All criminals should be locked up forever, or we should put more money into rehabilitating criminals, or we should accept that our streets will never be safe, or we should have a system for monitoring ex-convicts. We can't lock up all criminals forever, because it would be too expensive. We definitely won't accept that our streets will never be safe. So either we should put more money into rehabilitating criminals, or we should have some system for monitoring ex-convicts.
   Analysis   The first sentence is all one claim; it has the form: A or B or C or D. So the

argument as a whole is valid: A or B or C or D; not A; not C; therefore B or D. Whether it's good depends on whether the premises are plausible.

Remember: valid ≠ good. An argument that excludes possibilities is good only if its premises are plausible. We'll label the mistake we need to avoid.

> **False dilemma** A false dilemma is a bad use of excluding possibilities where the "or" claim is false or implausible. Sometimes just the dubious "or" claim is called a "false dilemma".

Example 11 Zoe: Look at these bills! You're either going to have to quit buying those nasty expensive cigars or get rid of your stupid dog Spot.
    Dick: What are you talking about? We can't get rid of Spot.
    Zoe: So you agree; you'll give up smoking those cigars.
    Analysis This is a false dilemma. Dick and Zoe could economize by not dining out.

Example 12 "Society can choose high environmental quality but only at the cost of lower tourism or more tourism and commercialization at the expense of the ecosystem, but society must choose. It involves a tradeoff."
    Analysis This is a false *exclusive* dilemma: The alternatives are claimed to be mutually exclusive. But Costa Rica has created a lot of tourism by preserving almost 50% of its land in parks. When you see a *versus*-claim, think "Is this a false dilemma?"

Now we will turn to claims compounded of others using "if . . . then . . ." .

> **Conditional claim**   A conditional is a claim that is or can be rewritten as an "if . . . then . . ." claim that must have the same truth-value.
>
> **Antecedent and consequent** In a conditional (rewritten as) "If A, then B", the claim A is the antecedent, and the claim B is the consequent.

Conditional claims are the most difficult kind we'll study, since they involve reasoning about possibilities. Here are some examples to work through to learn how to spot the parts of conditionals and the different ways we can make conditional claims.

Example 13 If the Mets win the World Series, the Dow Jones index will go up at least 2%.
    Analysis This is a conditional. Its antecedent is "The Mets win the World Series."
Its consequent is "The Dow Jones index will go up at least 2%."

Example 14 The economy will have positive growth this year if interest rates are lowered this week.
    Analysis This is a conditional. Its antecedent is "Interest rates are lowered this week."
Its consequent is "The economy will have positive growth this year."

Example 15 If Maria got a raise, then she wasn't late at all last month.

Analysis   This is a conditional with antecedent "Maria got a raise" and consequent "Maria wasn't late at all last month." The consequent need not happen later.

Example 16   Bring me an ice cream cone and I'll be happy.
    Analysis   This is a conditional with antecedent "You bring me an ice cream cone" and consequent "I'll be happy."

Example 17   Getting an 'A' in economics means you passed every test.
    Analysis   This is a conditional with antecedent "You get an 'A' in economics" and consequent "You passed every test."

Example 18   "A forecast is 'unbiased' if it contains no systematic forecasting errors."
    Analysis   This is not a compound claim; the word "if" here indicates a definition.

Example 19   Maria will not get rich since she hasn't invested in any tech stocks.
    Analysis   This is not a conditional; it's not even a compound claim. The word "since" indicates it is an argument with a single premise.

Example 20   If the Federal Reserve Board raises interest rates, then either inflation is above 3% or the President put pressure on the Chairman of the Board.
    Analysis   This is a conditional that has a compound claim as its consequent.

> **Contradictory of a conditional**   *If A, then B* has contradictory *A, but not B.*
> The contradictory of a conditional is not another conditional.

Example 21   If the minimum wage is raised, then there will be inflation.
    Contradictory   The minimum wage is raised, but there isn't any inflation.

Example 22   If interest rates are lowered, then employment will not fall.
    Contradictory   Interest rates are lowered, but unemployment does fall.

Example 23   Bring me an ice cream cone and I'll be happy.
    Contradictory   Despite that you brought me an ice cream cone, I'm not happy.
"Despite that" can also be used to make a contradictory of a conditional.

The following example will help you remember that the contradictory of a conditional is *not* another conditional.

Example 24   If the President gives a speech on the economy today, then General Motors will declare a dividend.
    Contradictory   The President gives a speech on the economy today, but General Motors does not declare a dividend.
    Not contradictory   If the President doesn't give a speech on the economy today, then General Motors will declare a dividend. (Both the example and this could be true if General Motors declares a dividend regardless of what the President says.)
    Not contradictory   If the President gives a speech on the economy today, then General Motors won't declare a dividend. (Both the example and this could be true by default if the President doesn't give a speech on the economy today.)
    Not contradictory   If the President doesn't give a speech on the economy today, then General Motors won't declare a dividend.

Given a conditional, however, we can form an equivalent one using "not".

> **Contrapositive**   The contrapositive of *If A, then B* is *If not B, then not A.*
> The contrapositive is true exactly when the original conditional is true.

Example 25   If interest rates go down, then unemployment will go down.
   Contrapositive   "If unemployment doesn't go down, then interest rates won't go down."
The original conditional gives a condition for unemployment to go down.   So if it didn't go down, then that condition must not have been true.

You should also be aware that "only if" does not mean the same as "if".

> **Only if *claims***   *A only if B* means the same as   *If not B, then not A.*

Example 26   The economy will have negative growth this year only if there is a war.
   Analysis   This example *means the same as* "If there is no war, then the economy will not have negative growth this year."

Conditionals are crucial for understanding what we mean by necessary or sufficient conditions.   For example, what's necessary for getting a driver's license?   You have to pass the driving exam.   That is: If you don't pass the driving exam, you won't get a driver's license.   There's no way you'll get a driver's license if you don't pass the driver's exam. You'll get a driver's license *only if* you pass the driving exam.
   On the other hand, what's sufficient for getting money at the bank?   Cashing a check there will do.   That is: If you cash a check at the bank, then you'll get money at the bank.

> **Necessary and sufficient conditions**
> A is *necessary* for B   means   "If not A, then not B" must be true.
> A is *sufficient* for B   means   "If A, then B" must be true.

Example 27   Passing an eye test is necessary but not sufficient for getting a driver's license.
   Analysis   This is the same as saying: "If you don't pass an eye test, you can't get a driver's license" is true, but "If you pass an eye test, you get a driver's license" need not be true.

Example 28   The essential condition for the existence and sway of the bourgeois class is the formation and augmentation of capital.
                                                    Marx and Engels, *Manifesto of the Communist Party*
   Analysis   Marx and Engels are asserting necessary (essential) but not sufficient conditions: If there is a bourgeois class that is in power, then there has been formation and augmentation of capital.   But the formation and augmentation of capital is not a sufficient condition for the existence of a bourgeois class that is in power, as we can see from the example of the former Soviet Union or China today.

Confusing "only if" with "if" is to confuse necessary with sufficient conditions.

Example 29   You can pass economics only if you study hard.
   Analysis   This isn't the same as "If you study hard, you can pass economics." Rather, studying hard is necessary (required) to pass economics. It's not sufficient.

There are some simple valid forms of reasoning using conditionals that are useful for analyzing and making arguments. There are also two similar weak forms that you need to be able to recognize. For example, suppose all the following conditionals are true:

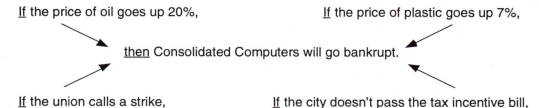

Ⅰf the price of oil goes up 20%,   Ⅰf the price of plastic goes up 7%,

then Consolidated Computers will go bankrupt.

Ⅰf the union calls a strike,   Ⅰf the city doesn't pass the tax incentive bill,

Example 30   If the union calls a strike, then Consolidated Computers will go bankrupt. The union called a strike. So Consolidated Computers went bankrupt.
   Analysis   This is a valid argument.

Example 31   If the union calls a strike, then Consolidated Computers will go bankrupt. Consolidated Computers didn't go bankrupt. So the union didn't call a strike.
   Analysis   This is a valid argument.

Example 32   If the price of oil goes up 20%, then Consolidated Computers will go bankrupt. The price of oil went up only 6%. So Consolidated Computers didn't go bankrupt.
   Analysis   This is an invalid and weak argument. Even when the price of oil doesn't go up 20%, Consolidated Computers can still go bankrupt if the price of plastic rises 9% or the city doesn't pass the tax incentive bill. This argument overlooks possibilities.

Example 33   If the price of plastic goes up 7%, then Consolidated Computers will go bankrupt. Consolidated Computers went bankrupt. So the price of plastic went up 7%.
   Analysis   This is an invalid and weak argument. The price of plastic going up 7% is only one way that Consolidated Computers could have gone bankrupt. Perhaps the price of oil rose 20% or the city didn't pass the tax incentive bill. This argument also overlooks possibilities.

These arguments illustrate the following general forms of reasoning with conditionals:

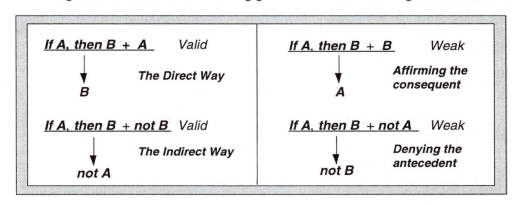

If A, then B + A *Valid*	**If A, then B + B** *Weak*
↓ ***The Direct Way***	↓ ***Affirming the consequent***
B	***A***
If A, then B + not B *Valid*	**If A, then B + not A** *Weak*
↓ ***The Indirect Way***	↓ ***Denying the antecedent***
not A	***not B***

The direct way of reasoning with conditionals is sometimes called *modus ponens*; the indirect way of reasoning with conditionals is sometimes called *modus tollens*.

Example 34   If Maria doesn't call Manuel, then Manuel will miss his class. Maria did call Manuel. So Manuel didn't miss his class.

   Analysis   This is invalid, an example of denying the antecedent, though the contradictories don't use "not". Schematically: *If* <u>Maria doesn't call Manuel</u>, *then* <u>Manuel will miss his class</u>.
   A   B

<u>Maria did call Manuel</u>.   *So* <u>Manuel didn't miss his class</u>.
not A   not B

Example 35   If there isn't inflation, then interest rates won't go up. Interest rates went up, so there was inflation.

   Analysis   This is a valid argument, using the indirect way of reasoning with conditionals. Neither contradictory here uses "not".

The invalid forms listed in the chart above are obvious confusions with valid forms, mistakes a good reasoner doesn't make. When you see one, *don't bother to repair the argument*.

Example 36   If the union calls a strike, then Consolidated Computers will go bankrupt. So Consolidated Computers didn't go bankrupt.

   Analysis   The obvious premise to add is "The union didn't call a strike." But that makes the argument weak. The argument is unrepairable.

Here's another valid form of reasoning with conditionals.

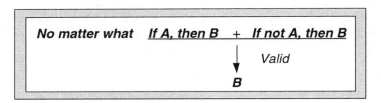

Example 37   If General Motors doesn't declare a dividend today, its stock will go lower. But if it does declare a dividend, it will be so small that its stock will go lower. So General Motors' stock will go lower no matter what.

   Analysis   This is valid, but whether it's good depends on whether the premises are plausible.

We can also reason in a chain with conditionals. We go little by little: If A, then B; if B, then C; . . . So if A is true, the last consequent is true too.

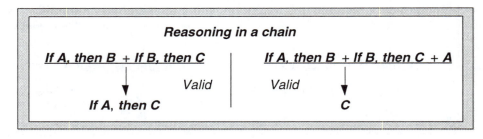

Example 38 If unemployment is reported today as having gone up, the stock market will go down at least 2%. If the stock market goes down 2%, then Dick's investments will lose $175. So if unemployment is reported as going up today, Dick's investments will lose $175.

Analysis This is an example of reasoning in a chain with conditionals. If the premises are true, then the conclusion, which is another conditional, is true.

Example 39 The government is going to spend less on health and welfare. If the government is going to spend less on health and welfare, then either the government is going to cut the Medicare budget or the government is going to slash spending on housing. If the government is going to cut the Medicare budget, the elderly will protest. If the government is going to slash spending on housing, then advocates for the poor will protest. Therefore, the elderly will protest or the advocates for the poor will protest.

Analysis This is a valid argument, which you can check by outlining its form in terms of conditionals and "or"-claims.

However, we can reason badly with a chain of conditionals.

> **Slippery slope** A slippery slope argument is a bad argument that uses a chain of conditionals, at least one of which is false or dubious.

Example 40 Don't get a credit card! If you do, you'll be tempted to spend money you don't have. Then you'll max out on your card. Then you'll be in real debt. And you'll have to drop out of school to pay your bills. You'll end up a failure in life.

Analysis You can see that this is reasoning in a chain with conditionals by rewriting each of the premises as a conditional. But it is a slippery slope, a bad argument.

Often when we reason about possibilities, we're not sure if they're true but we want to see what follows from them. That's hypothetical reasoning, and it's closely connected to reasoning with conditionals.

> **Reasoning from hypotheses** The following are equivalent:
> • Start with an hypothesis A and make a good argument for B.
> • Make a good argument for "If A, then B".

Example 41 Lee: I'm thinking of majoring in economics.
Maria: That means you'll take summer school. Here's why: You're in your second year now. To finish in four years like you told me you need to, you'll have to take all the upper-division econ courses your last two years. And you can't take any of those until you've finished the two-semester calculus course and statistics. So you'll have to take calculus over the summer in order to finish in four years.

Analysis Maria has not proved that Lee has to go to summer school. Rather, on the assumption (hypothesis) that Lee will major in economics, Lee will have to go to summer school. That is, Maria has proved: If Lee majors in economics, then he'll have to go to summer school.

3.2 Counterarguments

In this section we'll learn how to raise objections and answer them in our reasoning, which will lead to how to refute an argument or claim.

Example 1
> Dick: Zoe, we ought to get another dog.
> Zoe: What's wrong with Spot?
> Dick: Oh, no, I mean to keep Spot company.
> Zoe: Spot has us. He doesn't need company.
> Dick: But we're gone a lot. And he's always escaping from the yard, 'cause he's lonely. And we don't give him enough time. He should be out running around more.
> Zoe: But think of all the work! We'll have to feed the new dog. And think of all the time necessary to train it.
> Dick: I'll train him. We can feed him at the same time as Spot, and dog food is cheap. It won't cost much.

Analysis Dick is trying to convince Zoe to believe "We should get another dog." But he has to answer her objections.

> We ought to get another dog.
>   (*objection*) We already have Spot.
> The other dog will keep Spot company. (*answer*)
>   (*objection*) Spot already has us for company.
> We are gone a lot. (*answer*)
> He is always escaping from the yard. (*answer*)
> He's lonely. (*answer*)
> We don't give him enough time. (*answer*)
> He should be out running around more. (*answer*)
>   (*objection*) It will be a lot of work to have a new dog.
>   (*objection*) We will have to feed the new dog.
>   (*objection*) It will take a lot of time to train the new dog.
> I (Dick) will train him. (*answer*)
> We can feed him at the same time as Spot. (*answer*)
> Dog food is cheap. (*answer*)

Argument. Counterargument. Counter-counterargument. Objections are raised. Someone puts forward a claim that, if true, makes one of our claims false or at least doubtful. We then have to answer that challenge to sustain our argument.

> *Knocking off an objection is a mini-argument within your argument—if it's not a good (though brief) argument, it won't do the job.*

But reasoning well doesn't mean always winning. You could say to an objection, *I hadn't thought of that, I guess you're right.* Or you could say, *I don't know, I'll have to think about that.*

In making an argument, you'll want to make it good. You might think you have a great one. All the premises seem obvious and they lead to the conclusion. But if you imagine someone objecting, you can see how to give better support for doubtful premises or make it clearer that the argument is valid or strong. Just make a list of the pros and cons. Then answer the other side.

All the ways that we can show an argument is unrepairable are useful in refuting an argument. We pick out three as fundamental.

Direct ways of refuting an argument

1. Show that at least one of the premises is false.

2. Show that the argument isn't valid or strong.

3. Show that the conclusion is false.

Example 2 It's useless to kill flies. The ones you kill will be the slowest, because the fastest ones will evade you. Over time, then, the genes for being fast will predominate. Then with super-fast flies, it will be impossible to kill them anyway. So it's useless to kill flies.

To refute this argument: We might object to one of the premises, saying that you won't be killing the slowest ones, but only the ones that happen to come into your house.

Or we might accept the premises, but note that "over time" could be thousands of years, so the conclusion doesn't follow.

Or we could attack the conclusion directly, pointing out that we kill flies all the time and it keeps the house clean.

Or we can refute an argument indirectly by the following method.

Reducing to the absurd This is a way to refute a claim or an argument by showing that at least one of several claims is false or dubious, or collectively they are unacceptable, by drawing a false or unwanted conclusion from them.

If a valid argument has a false conclusion, one of the premises is false. If a strong argument has a false conclusion, one of the premises is very likely false. If the conclusion is absurd, the premises aren't what you want.

Example 3 You complain that taxes are already too high and there is too much crime. And you say we should permanently lock up everyone who has been convicted of three felonies. In the places where this has been instituted, it hasn't reduced the crime rate. So we will have many, many more people who will be incarcerated for their entire lives. We will need more prisons, many more, because these people will be in forever. We will need to employ more guards. We will need to pay for a lot of healthcare for these people when they are elderly. Thus, if you lock up everyone who has been convicted of three felonies, we will have to pay substantially higher taxes. Since you are adamant that taxes are too high, you should abandon your claim that we should permanently lock up everyone who has been convicted of three felonies.

Analysis Here the speaker is showing that the claims that taxes are too high and we should permanently lock up everyone who has been convicted of three felonies lead to a contradiction. So the other person should give up one of those.

When you use this method, be sure that the argument you use to get the false or absurd conclusion is good. Otherwise it may be the claims you introduce or the weakness of the argument you make that give the contradiction.

One particular form of reducing to the absurd is called **refuting by analogy**: Vary only some of the premises while retaining the crucial ones to get an absurd conclusion. For example, we could respond to Example 2 by saying, "Your argument against killing flies is bad. We could use the same argument against killing bacteria or against killing chickens for dinner from a farmer's henhouse. Those conclusions would be absurd."

There are several ways to try to refute that are themselves bad. We've already seen *phony refutations* and *slippery slope arguments*. In addition, there is **ridicule**. Ridicule is a worthless device: it ends a discussion, belittles your opponent, and makes enemies.

Example 4 Dr. E: I hear that your department elected a woman as chairman.

Professor Bilrabi: That's right. Now we're trying to decide what we should call her— "chairman" or "chairwoman" or "chairperson."

Dr. E: "Chairperson"? Why not use a neutral term that's really appropriate for the position, like "chaircreature"?

Analysis No argument has been given for why "chairman" shouldn't be replaced by "chairperson", although Dr. E thinks he's shown the idea is ridiculous.

Finally, there's the following all-purpose way to evade another person's argument.

Strawman A bad way to refute by putting words in your opponent's mouth.

Example 5 Tom: Unless we allow the logging of old-growth forests in this county, we'll lose the timber industry and these towns will die.

Dick: So you're saying that you don't care what happens to the spotted owl and to our rivers and the water we drink?

Tom: I said nothing of the sort. You've misrepresented my position.

Analysis The only reasonable response to a strawman is to say, "That isn't what I said."

The following letter to the editor shows how important it is to master these methods and not just bluster; it didn't convince a lot of people.

Should you decide you are interested in supplying your readers with something other than lies and bullshit, I suggest you spend more time fact checking for yourself. This will help prevent you from the embarrassment of propagating others' inaccuracies.

Vern Raburn, CEO, Eclipse Aviation, Albuquerque
letter to the editor, *Crosswinds Weekly*, July 11, 2002

3.3 General Claims

In this section we'll look at claims that assert something in a general
way about a part of a collection using the words "all", "some", and "none".
We'll learn how to form contradictories of those kind of claims and how
to recognize some typical forms of arguments that are valid or weak.

All means "Every single one, no exceptions".
  Sometimes *all* is meant as "Every single one, and there is at least one".
Some means "At least one".
  Sometimes *some* is meant as "At least one, but not all".

Which of these readings is best depends on how the words are used in an argument.

Example 1 All CEOs are human.
  Analysis This is a true claim.

Example 2 All bank managers are women.
  Analysis This is a false claim on either reading of "all".

Example 3 All polar bears in Antarctica can swim.
  Analysis This is a true claim if you understand "all" as "every single one". It is false if you
understand "all" to mean also "at least one", since there aren't any polar bears in Antarctica.

Example 4 Some CEOs are women.
  Analysis This is a true claim on either reading of "some".

Example 5 Some CEOs are human.
  Analysis This is a true claim if you understand "some" to mean "at least one". But it's false
if you understand "some" to include "but not all".

There are lots of different ways to say "all" in English. For example, the following are
equivalent claims:

  All dogs bark.   Dogs bark.   Every dog barks.   Everything that's a dog barks.

There are lots of ways to say the first reading of "some" in English. For example, the
following are equivalent claims:

  Some dogs can't bark.   At least one dog can't bark.   There is a dog that can't bark.

There are also lots of ways of saying that **none** of a collection or **nothing** satisfies
some condition. For example, the following are equivalent claims:

No dog likes cats.   All dogs do not like cats.   Not even one dog likes cats.

Just as we have to be careful with "only if", we need to take care with "only".

Example 6   Only bank employees can open the vault at this bank. Pete is a bank employee. So Pete can open the vault at this bank.
   Analysis   The premises are true, but the conclusion is false: Pete is the janitor at this bank. "Only" does not mean "all". "Only bank employees can open the vault" means "Anyone who can open the vault is a bank employee", that is, if you can open the vault, then you're a bank employee.

Only S are P means *All P are S.*

Here are some examples of contradictories of general claims.

Example 7   All people want to be rich. *Contradictory* Some people don't want to be rich.

Example 8   Some people want to fail. *Contradictory* No people want to fail.

Example 9   Some people don't want to be rich. *Contradictory* All people want to be rich.

Example 10   No women are CEOs. *Contradictory* Some women are CEOs.

Example 11   Every economist likes math. *Contradictory* Some economists don't like math.

Example 12   Some corporations have been indicted. *Contradictory* Not even one corporation has been indicted.

Example 13 Only accountants can audit Consolidated Computers. *Contradictory* Someone other than an accountant can audit Consolidated Computers.

Given the many ways to make claims using "all", "some", "no", and "only", the following is at best a rough guide for forming their contradictories:

Claim	Contradictory
All S are P	Some S are not P Not every S is P
Some S are P	No S are P All S are not P Not even one S is P
Some S are not P	All S are P
No S is P	Some S are P
Only S are P	Some P are not S Not every P is S

There are several methods that can help us determine whether an argument using general claims is valid or weak, which we describe in detail in our larger textbook *Critical Thinking*. Here we'll just contrast the most common valid forms with forms of weak arguments that are similar.

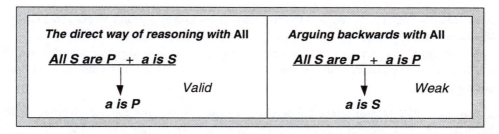

Example 14 All accountants are honest. Ralph is an accountant. So Ralph is honest.

    Analysis This is a valid argument, the direct way of reasoning. But it's a bad argument, since the first premise is false.

Example 15 All CEOs earn more than $50,000. Ralph earns more than $50,000. So Ralph is a CEO.

    Analysis This is weak, arguing backwards with "all". It overlooks other possibilities: Ralph could be a basketball player or a dentist.

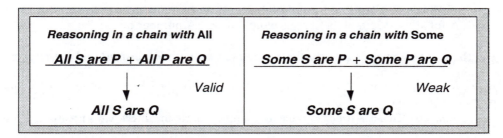

Example 16 All corporations are required to have an annual auditing. Everything that is required to have an annual auditing files a federal tax return. So all corporations file a federal tax return.

    Analysis This is valid, reasoning in a chain with "all".

Example 17 Some dogs like peanut butter. Some things that like peanut butter are human. So some dogs are human.

    Analysis This is weak, reasoning in a chain with "some".

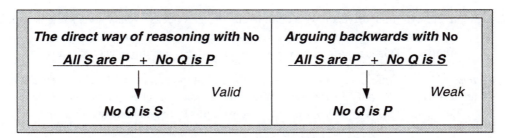

Example 18 All corporations are legal entities. No computer is a legal entity. So no computer is a corporation.

    Analysis This is valid, the direct way of reasoning with "no".

Example 19 All corporations file federal tax returns. No limited partnership is a corporation. So no limited partnership files federal tax returns.
    Analysis This is weak, arguing backwards with "no".

Arguments using *precise* generalities are often easy to evaluate.

Example 20 72% of all workers at the GM plant voted to strike. Harry works at the GM plant. So Harry voted to strike.
    Analysis We can say exactly where this argument lands on the strong-weak scale: There is a 28% chance the premises could be true and the conclusion false. That's not strong enough for a good argument.

Example 21 95% plus-or-minus 2% of all cat owners buy over-the-counter allergy medicines. Barbi has a cat. So very probably Barbi buys over-the-counter allergy medicines.
    Analysis This is a strong argument; "very probably" is only indicating the speaker's belief.

Example 22 Only 4% of all workers on the assembly line at the GM plant didn't get a raise last year. Wanda has worked on the assembly line at the GM plant for two years. So Wanda got a raise.
    Analysis This is a strong argument.

In comparison, the following words are usually too vague to use in a claim:

Most	Mostly	Many	A few
A lot	Quite a lot	A bunch of	A number of

But there are two vague generalities we can reason with: ***almost all*** and ***a very few***.

Example 23 Almost all CEOs are over thirty years old. So the CEO of Consolidated Computers is over thirty years old.
    Analysis This is a strong argument. Compare this to the direct way of reasoning with "all".

Example 24 Almost all university professors teach every year. Mary Jane teaches every year. So Mary Jane is a university professor.
    Analysis This is a weak argument. Mary Jane could be a high school teacher. Compare this to arguing backwards with "all".

Example 25 Almost all dogs like ice cream. Almost all things that like ice cream don't bark. So almost all dogs don't bark.
    Analysis This is a weak argument. We cannot reason in a chain with "almost all".

Example 26 All truck drivers have a commercial driver's license. Only a very few beauticians have a commercial driver's license. So only a very few beauticians are truck drivers.
    Analysis This is a strong argument. Compare this to the direct way of reasoning with "no".

Example 27 All professors get a paycheck at the end of the month. Only a very few people under 25 are professors. So only a very few people under 25 get a paycheck at the end of the month.
    Analysis This is a weak argument. Compare this to arguing backwards with "no".

Example 28 Very few economists believe that a communist economy is efficient. Reginald is an economist. So Reginald does not believe that a communist economy is efficient.
    Analysis This is a strong argument. Compare this to the direct way of reasoning with "no".

Here are some examples to help you learn how to determine whether an argument that uses general claims is valid or strong. For some you can refer to the forms above. But they all can be figured out if you return to the fundamentals: It's not whether the premises and conclusion happen to be true; rather, is there any possible way the premises could be true and the conclusion false, and if so, is such a way likely?

Example 29 Every newspaper that Maria reads is published by an American publisher. All newspapers published by an American publisher are biased against Muslims. So Maria reads only newspapers that are biased against Muslims.

Analysis This is a valid argument, reasoning in a chain with "all", but whether it is good depends on whether the premises are plausible.

Example 30 Everyone who wants to become a manager works hard. The people in Jennifer's group work hard. So the people in Jennifer's group want to become managers.

Analysis This is a weak argument, reasoning backwards: Maybe the workers in Jennifer's group just want a raise and not the responsibility.

Example 31 No bank CFO makes less than $100,000. Some employees who make over $100,000 are women. So some bank CFOs are women.

Analysis This is a weak argument: Perhaps the women who make more than $100,000 are all Human Resource Directors. That the conclusion is true doesn't make the argument good.

Example 32 Some bosses yell at their employees. Some employees yell at their bosses. So some bosses and employees yell at each other.

Analysis This is weak: Maybe all the employees who yell at bosses are afraid to yell at the bosses who will yell back at them.

Example 33 Some Federal Reserve Board members are women. Some women have earned a B.A. So some Federal Reserve Board members have earned a B.A.

Analysis This is weak and hence bad, even though the premises and the conclusion are true. It's reasoning in a chain with "some".

Example 34 No CFO of a Fortune 500 company is unaware of accounting irregularities in his company. Scott Sullivan was the CFO of WorldCom. So Scott Sullivan was aware of WorldCom's accounting irregularities.

Analysis This is a valid argument, using the direct way of reasoning with "no". But it's bad, since we don't have good reason to believe the first premise.

Example 35 All CFOs have an accounting degree. No heroin addict is a CFO. So no heroin addict has an accounting degree.

Analysis This is weak, arguing backwards with "no".

Example 36 Some employees don't have health insurance. Maria is an employee. So Maria doesn't have health insurance.

Analysis This is invalid and weak.

Example 37 Every employee pays Social Security tax. Dr. E is not an employee. So Dr. E does not pay Social Security tax.

Analysis This is weak. Dr. E could be self-employed and pay Social Security tax.

Example 38 No one who reads this book is going to beg in the street because only poor people beg. And people who read this book won't be poor because they understand how to reason well.

Analysis This is a terrific argument. Trust us.

3.4 Normative Claims

Economists talk about not only what is, but what ought to be. In this section we'll see that reasoning about values depends on first establishing standards.

> **Normative and positive claims**   A claim is *positive* if it says what is. A claim is *normative* if it says what should be.

Positive claims are also called *descriptive*; normative claims are called *prescriptive*. Every claim is either positive or normative.

Example 1 No limited partnership is a corporation.
  Analysis This is a positive claim.

Example 2 Dick: I am hot.
  Zoe: You should take your sweater off.
  Analysis Dick makes a positive claim. *Positive claims can be either subjective or objective.* Zoe responds with a normative claim.

Example 3 The government must not legalize marijuana.
  Analysis This is a normative claim, using "must" to indicate "should".

Example 4 The Federal Reserve Board ought to lower interest rates.
  Analysis This is a normative claim.

Example 5 There will be inflation in the first quarter of next year.
  Analysis This is a positive claim. It describes the world, asserting what "is" in the future.

The words "good", "better", "best" and "bad", "worse", "worst" and other value judgments are normative when they carry with them the unstated assumption: "If it's good (preferable, . . .), then we (you) should do it; if it's bad, we (you) shouldn't do it."

Example 6 A rise in prices will cause a drop in demand.
  Analysis This is a positive claim.

Example 7 A rise in prices will be bad for the economy.
  Analysis This is a normative claim, since we should not do what is bad.

We cannot deduce a normative claim from positive claims only, for a standard of values is first needed. That is, a prescriptive claim cannot be derived from premises all of which are descriptive. "Is" does not imply "ought".

> *Every normative claim either gives a standard or assumes another normative claim as the standard.*

Example 8 Smoking destroys people's health. So we ought to raise the tax on cigarettes.

   Analysis The premise, which is a positive claim, is true, as we discuss in Section 4.6. But the conclusion does not follow without some normative premise such as "We should tax activities that are destructive of people's health." Why we should believe that is then the issue.

Example 9 The Federal Reserve Bank should raise interest rates in order to keep inflation low.

   Analysis This is really two normative claims: "The Federal Reserve Bank should raise interest rates" and then a reason why in terms of a standard, "We should keep inflation low."

Example 10 The government should raise the tax rate for the upper 1% of all taxpayers.

   Analysis This is a normative claim. Before we can judge whether it's true, we need to know what standard lies behind that "should": What is a good method of taxation?

Example 11 It's wrong to murder people.

   Analysis This is a normative claim. It's usually taken as a standard, rather than assuming another standard.

Example 12 Tom: Capitalism is good because it raises the average income of everyone.

   Analysis This is a normative claim: "good" here has to be understood as implying the system should be adopted. Tom might say that by "good economic system" he just means one that raises the average income of everyone in the society, but that would be a persuasive definition: The issue is whether that's what we think a good economic system should be.

Example 13 You say that the income tax deduction for home mortgage interest is unfair to the poor because they can't use it. But you say that the earned income tax deduction is fair even though the middle class can't use it. So where do you draw the line? Your notion of fairness is too vague for me to understand.

   Analysis To evaluate normative claims about fairness, a standard is needed. But, as is often the case, that standard may be informal and quite difficult to make explicit. It's a drawing the line fallacy to say that if we can't make the notion absolutely precise, there is no usable notion.

Example 14 I totally don't support prohibiting smoking in bars—most people who go to bars do smoke and people should be aware that a bar is a place where a lot of people go to have a drink and smoke. There are no youth working or attending bars and I just don't believe you can allow people to go have a beer but not to allow people to have a cigarette—that's a person's God-given right.

                    Gordy Hicks, City Councilor, Socorro, N.M., reported in *El Defensor Chieftain*

   Analysis The implicit standard here for why smoking shouldn't be prohibited in bars seems to be that society should not establish sanctions against any activity that doesn't corrupt youth or create harm to others who can't avoid it. The argument is just as good without the appeal to God, so by the Guide to Repairing Arguments we can ignore that. If it turns out that Hicks really does think the standard is theological, then the argument he gave isn't adequate.

Example 15 (Two passages from the same book)
(1) "In trying to make themselves better off, people alter their behavior if the expected marginal benefits from doing so outweigh the expected marginal costs—this is the rule of rational choice."
(2) "*Rule of rational choice* Individuals should pursue an activity as long as the expected marginal benefits are greater than the expected marginal costs."

   Analysis The author has presented the rule of rational choice as a positive claim ("people alter their behavior if . . .") and as a normative standard ("individuals should pursue . . ."). But it can't be both.

People who think that all normative claims are subjective are called *relativists*: What's right for me need not be right for you; there are no absolute standards of value.

Example 16 "The problem with all these criteria is that the choice among them seems entirely arbitrary. [The author cites various conflicting standards on which to base economic policy.] . . . I suspect though that the choice of a normative criterion is ultimately a matter of taste."

Analysis This author seems to be a relativist. But he might just be committing the subjectivist fallacy, mistaking lack of agreement for subjectivity.

Most people believe that at least some normative claims are objective, such as "Murder is wrong." And almost everyone believes that the choice is not arbitrary.

Economists divide their study into two parts. *Positive economics* is an attempt to describe the world and make predictions about what will happen based on observations. *Normative economics* is an attempt to establish standards for what is good or bad for societies, or companies, or individuals to do in the domain of economic choices, that is, economic policy. Normative economics requires standards that are, in the end, statements of ethical views about what is best for a person or society.

Example 17 "Almost all economists believe that rent control adversely affects the availability and quality of housing and is a very costly way of helping the most needy members of society. Nonetheless, many city governments choose to ignore the advice of economists and place ceilings on the rents that landlords may charge their tenants."

Analysis That "nonetheless" slips in a value judgment that city governments shouldn't adopt a policy that adversely affects availability and quality of housing and is a costly way of helping the most needy members of society. You may agree, but you need to be aware that in doing so you're accepting a normative standard.

Example 18 "In his criticisms of the North American Free Trade Agreement, Perot was quick to cite estimates of its potential for reducing wages and employment. His two opponents [in the election for President of the U.S.], declared supporters of the agreement, chose to play on Perot's turf by disputing his estimates. They never came close to articulating a truly appropriate response by citing estimates of the agreement's potential for reducing the prices of consumer goods and expanding the array of goods available. If the effect of the agreement is that Americans work less and consume more, we win."

Analysis This passage establishes the author's normative standard: What is best is what in sum total averaged over all people in a society leads to less work and more consumption. This is in contrast to other standards, such as that the best policy is one that improves the welfare of the least well-off people in a society. The author does not defend his view, taking it as a given of economics, yet many economists disagree.

Economists can differ on:

1. Assumptions about how economies work
2. Evidence
3. Goals
4. Means

"Goals" are determined by the normative standards they hold. Items (3) and (4) are policy issues, while (1) and (2) are the basis of economics as a descriptive science. We expect there to be disagreement about goals. But we also have a right to expect that disagreement to be reasoned, based on knowledge of and deliberation about various ethical alternatives.

Example 19 "The arguments against universal entitlements center on their expense and their potential for disincentives. Opponents ask, for example, why the government should fund child care for all, rather than just for low-income families in need. And if child allowances provide cash income based on the number of children per family, won't the allowances cause the birth rate to increase?

Proponents reject these claims. They argue that the political likelihood of enacting and maintaining programs and policies is much greater if such programs benefit all, rather than just the poor. Furthermore, only if programs providing benefits such as medical care and child care are targeted to all will quality be ensured; programs for only the poor have often been of substandard quality."

Analysis In this passage, consequences of particular economic choices are cited in favor of or against the claim "Universal entitlements are good (should be adopted by the government)." But what may be considered a bad consequence for one side could be a good consequence from the other point of view. Without knowing the normative standards adopted by the two sides, the debate is fruitless.

Example 20 "Here is an important reminder: Don't confuse efficiency with fairness. Producing the quantity of a good where the demand and supply curves intersect will be *efficient*, but it may not be *fair*.

To see why, remember that the demand—or marginal benefit—curve tells us how much income some consumer would give up to buy another unit of a good. But this, in turn, depends on how much income the consumer *has*. A very poor person might want food very badly, but if she has no income, her desire would not register at all on the demand curve. Thus, in principle, an efficient level of food production could be one in which many people starve, and just a few—those with income—have food.

More generally, the market demand curve for any good will depend on the distribution of income and wealth in the society. If that distribution is regarded as unfair, then the quantities of goods produced and consumed will be unfair as well, even though they may be efficient."

Analysis This is a careful statement of how economic theory does not necessarily yield economic policy: Whether an efficient choice is good depends on moral considerations.

Example 21 We need to elect Schwartz as governor. He has the experience of running a big company and that qualifies him to run this state.

Analysis This assumes a normative claim: We should have business executives running our government *because* they know how to run organizations efficiently. But economic efficiency is only part of a normative standard for what counts as good governance. Business executives do not typically have to decide between competing normative standards; politicians do.

Example 22 "*Cost benefit analysis* is the systematic comparison of all the costs of a program with all of the benefits. The program should be undertaken only if the benefits are greater than the costs. From the perspective of the environment, let's look at the costs and benefits of environmental protection programs. The costs of these programs are the costs incurred by government in regulating business, in running public recycling programs, and in any other activity that cuts down on or cleans up pollution. Business firms also incur costs of environmental protection. If they adopt a more expensive but less polluting process, their increase in cost is an environmental protection cost. If they use less polluting but more costly raw materials, the difference in cost is also an environmental protection cost. If they install and maintain pollution control equipment, such as scrubbers in smokestacks, they incur an environmental protection cost. Consumers can also incur environmental protection costs if they install high-efficiency, less polluting furnaces and other appliances, or if they incur the expense and inconvenience of recycling. The environmental protection costs are the total of all these costs, whether incurred by government, business, or households.

The benefits of environmental protection are the improvements in our environmental quality that result. Some of these benefits are quantifiable. We save on cleaning costs if air pollution is reduced. Businesses save on repair costs when acid rain no longer damages their structures. We save on medical costs when people no longer suffer the ill health that results from pollution.

However, many of the benefits of environmental programs cannot be calculated in monetary terms. The personal benefits of improved health and longevity go far beyond the savings on medical costs. The biodiversity of our rain forests is expected to yield yet-undiscovered products to benefit humankind. And there is no way to place a price on a stream used for trout fishing or a lake used for swimming that might otherwise be too polluted for use.

In reconciling the costs with the benefits of environmental protection, we must take a wide view and a long view. We must consider the monetary and nonmonetary benefits of environmental protection, and we must consider the benefits to future as well as current generations."

Analysis The authors here are clear about what counts as marginal benefits and marginal costs. Many economists would disagree, however, that no monetary figure could be given for the biodiversity of our rainforests or an unpolluted lake. Every day figures are assigned to such resources by economists, usually in terms of how much a person is willing to pay to get something or to avoid something else.

But even if all these nonmonetary benefits are factored in, to say that we should choose a course of action in which costs and benefits are balanced is to give a normative standard that is only one among many. Compare: Someone may be willing to sell himself into slavery if $10,000,000 is given to his family, and he may well be worth that much to someone. But our society does not allow it, even if the person thought the benefits were equal to the costs, because we take as an absolute moral standard that no person should be a slave. We could adopt another standard on environmental pollution: Lower pollution so that absolutely no one in the society will become ill due to enforced exposure to toxic chemicals, based on the normative standard that society must protect everyone, especially the weak. Alternatively, we could adopt a standard that says we should not impose any restrictions on polluting so long as those not doing the polluting can avoid the pollution if they wish, for individual rights are what is most important (compare Example 14 above): No monetary value can be given to how much we value private rights or the protection of the poor if those are absolute standards. The cost-benefit analysis for a *society* carries with it a normative assumption that we should do what will bring the greatest good to the greatest number of people, which is only one of many normative standards. It cannot resolve fundamental moral disputes about rights and protections.

Example 23 Positive economics is in principle independent of any particular ethical position or normative judgments. As Keynes says, it deals with 'what is,' not with 'what ought to be.' Its task is to provide a system of generalizations that can be used to make correct predictions about the consequences of any change in circumstances. Its performance is to be judged by the precision, scope, and conformity with experience of the predictions it yields. In short, positive economics is, or can be, an "objective" science, in precisely the same sense as any of the physical sciences. . . .

Normative economics and the art of economics, on the other hand, cannot be independent of positive economics. Any policy conclusion necessarily rests on a prediction about the consequences of doing one thing rather than another, a prediction that must be based—implicitly or explicitly—on positive economics.   Milton Friedman, "The methodology of positive economics"

Analysis Friedman here is adopting a particular normative view: We judge whether actions are good or bad by their consequences. Someone who does not believe that the ends justify the means could very well hold that normative economics is (at least in some instances) independent of positive economics. For example, we don't investigate the consequences of outlawing slavery to adopt that as an economic policy; we simply say it is wrong. Pragmatism is just one of many ethical standards.

4 Reasoning about Experience

In reasoning about the world we draw comparisons, we use numbers and graphs, we generalize, we try to determine cause and effect. Those kinds of reasoning require special skills. There are particular problems we should avoid and certain methods that will help us better understand the world.

In Section 4.1 we look at how to reason using comparisons. Analogies are typically incomplete arguments, but investigating them carefully can lead us to clarify our thinking.

In Sections 4.2 we look at how numbers can be misused in making claims, and in Section 4.3 we look at how we can be misled by badly drawn graphs.

Section 4.4 is about how we can generalize from our experience, arriving at true claims about a group from knowing something about only a part of that group. We'll see how to avoid lots of mistakes in generalizing.

Section 4.5 is devoted to the main focus of much of economics: cause and effect. We'll see how to determine causes and how to avoid errors in reasoning about them. That will lead us to methods for determining causes from statistical evidence in Section 4.6.

4.1 Analogies

In this section we'll learn how to reason by using comparisons.

> **Analogies**   A comparison becomes reasoning by analogy when it is part of an argument: On one side of the comparison we draw a conclusion, so on the other side we say that we should conclude the same.

Example 1   We should legalize marijuana. After all, if we don't, what's the rationale for alcohol and tobacco being legal?
   Analysis   This is an analogy. Alcohol is legal. Tobacco is legal. Therefore, marijuana should be legal. They are sufficiently similar.

Example 2   DDT has been shown to cause cancer in rats. Therefore, there is a good chance DDT will cause cancer in humans.
   Analysis   This is an analogy. Rats are like humans. So if rats get cancer from DDT, so will humans.

Example 3   A university is like a company. Raising the prices drives away consumers. So the university shouldn't raise tuition if it wants to keep enrollment high.
   Analysis   This is an analogy. Universities are like companies; students are like consumers. If a company raises prices it will lose consumers, so if a university raises tuition, it will lose students.

   An analogy is typically an incomplete argument. It will rely on an unstated general principle. The value of an analogy is often uncovering that principle, making explicit what was only implicit. Here is an example that will illustrate the general method of evaluating analogies before we turn to analogies in economics.

Example 4   "Blaming soldiers for war is like blaming firemen for fires."
(Background: Country Joe MacDonald was a rock star who wrote songs protesting the war in Vietnam. In 1995 he was interviewed on National Public Radio about his motives for working to establish a memorial for Vietnam War soldiers in Berkeley, California, his home and a center of anti-war protests in the 60s and 70s. This claim was his response.)
   Analysis   This is a comparison. But it's meant as an argument:

   We don't blame firemen for fires.
   Firemen and fires are like soldiers and wars.
   Therefore, we should not blame soldiers for war.

In what way are firemen and fires like soldiers and wars? They have to be similar enough in some respect for Country Joe's remark to be more than suggestive. We need to pick out important similarities that we can use as premises.

Firemen and fires are like soldiers and war.

> wear uniforms
> answer to chain of command
> cannot disobey superior without serious consequences
> fight (fires/wars)
> work done when fire/war is over
> until recently only men
> lives at risk in work
> fire/war kills others
> firemen don't start fires—soldiers don't start wars
> usually like beer

That's stupid: Firemen and soldiers usually like beer. So?

When you ask "So?" you're on the way to deciding if the analogy is good. It's not just any similarity that's important. There must be some crucial, important way that firemen fighting fires is like soldiers fighting wars, some similarity that can account for why we don't blame firemen for fires that also applies to soldiers and war. Some of the similarities listed don't seem to matter. Others we can't use because they trade on an ambiguity, like saying firemen "fight" fires.

We don't have any good guide for how to proceed; that's a weakness of the original argument. But if we are to take Country Joe MacDonald's remark seriously, we have to come up with some principle that applies to both sides.

The similarities that seem most important are that both firemen and soldiers are involved in dangerous work, trying to end a problem/disaster they didn't start. We don't want to blame someone for helping to end a disaster that could harm us all.

(*)   Firemen are involved in dangerous work.
Soldiers are involved in dangerous work.
The job of a fireman is to end a fire.
The job of a soldier is to end a war.
Firemen don't start fires.
Soldiers don't start wars.

But even with these added to the original argument, we don't get a good argument for the conclusion that we shouldn't blame soldiers for wars. We need a general principle:

> You shouldn't blame someone for helping to end a disaster that could harm others—
> if he didn't start the disaster.

This general principle seems plausible and gives a valid argument.

But is the argument good? Are all the premises true? This is the point where the differences between firemen and soldiers might be important.

The first two premises at (*) are clearly true, and so is the third. But is the job of soldiers to end a war? And do soldiers really not start wars? Look at this difference:

> Without firemen there would still be fires.
> Without soldiers there wouldn't be any wars.

Without soldiers there would still be violence. But without soldiers—any soldiers anywhere— there could be no organized violence of one country against another.

So? The analogy shouldn't convince. The argument has a dubious premise.

We did not prove that soldiers *should* be blamed for wars. When you show an argument is bad you haven't proved the conclusion false. You've only shown that you have no more reason than before for believing the conclusion.

Perhaps the premises at (*) could be modified, using that soldiers are drafted for wars. But that's beyond Country Joe's argument. If he meant something more, then it's his responsibility to flesh it out. Or we could use his comparison as a starting place to decide whether there is a general principle, based on the similarities, for why we shouldn't blame soldiers for war.

Evaluating an analogy

1. Is this an argument? What is the conclusion?

2. What is the comparison?

3. What are the premises (the sides of the comparison)?

4. What are the similarities?

5. Can we state the similarities as premises and find a *general principle* that covers the two sides?

6. Does the general principle really apply to both sides? What about the differences?

7. Is the argument strong or valid? Is it good?

In Chapter 5 we'll see that scientists, and especially economists, use analogies in very precise ways when they create models that often yield very good arguments. That contrasts with the very loose way analogies are usually used.

Example 5   The first rule of a physician is to do no harm. Let the body use its own natural restorative powers. If a physician is uncertain about the correct diagnosis of a sick patient, he should do nothing and leave the patient's body to heal itself.

It's the same for an ailing economy. It would be great if policymakers could eliminate all economic fluctuations, but that's not a realistic goal given the limits of our knowledge of macro-economics and how unpredictable world events are. So economic policymakers, just as doctors, should often refrain from intervening with monetary and fiscal policy and be content if they do no harm.

Analysis   This is an analogy with conclusion, "Economic policymakers should often refrain from intervening with monetary and fiscal policy and be content if they do no harm." That is a normative claim. It follows from the general principle, "If you don't know for sure what's wrong and how to fix it, you should leave well enough alone."

The analogy compares an economy to a human body. What are the similarities? Like a human body, an economy has healthy and sick states. Intervening when there is an uncertain diagnosis can put the economy, just like a human body, into a worse state.

But the differences are significant. Human bodies can often cure themselves, but what evidence do we have that a "sick" economy can cure itself? Most importantly, though, is that we know what it means to say a human body is healthy or sick, but to say which states of an economy are healthy and which are sick is to set out a normative standard that is hardly obvious or noncontroversial.

The differences here are too great to suggest that the general principle really applies to both sides. But again, that doesn't mean the conclusion is false, only that this argument gives us no good reason to believe it.

Example 6 "Sometimes it is mistakenly believed that speculation can be avoided by legally imposing fixed prices on commodities. This is identical to painting the thermometer to avoid a fever. Price controls do not prevent shifts in demand or supply. They prevent the opportunity of people to adjust by exchange to differences in interpersonal values among goods as well as among risks."

Analysis This is not an analogy. The authors are only using a comparison to make their point more forcefully.

We often draw analogies between individuals and groups. But the differences between individuals and groups are usually too great for such an analogy to be good.

Example 7 What is prudence in the conduct of every private family, can scarce be folly in that of a great kingdom. If a foreign country can supply us with a commodity cheaper than we ourselves make it, better buy it of them with some part of the produce of our own industry, employed in a way in which we have some advantage.

Adam Smith, Wealth of Nations

Analysis A country is not like an individual: It may be difficult for an individual to learn how to produce a commodity more cheaply, but it might be easy for an industry within a country to become much more efficient with government protection. This does not show that Smith's conclusion is false, but that his analogy shouldn't convince you it's true.

Fallacy of composition It's a mistake to argue that what is true of the individual is therefore true of the group, or that what is true of the group is therefore true of the individual.

Example 8 "Economic theory clearly indicates that individual nations will benefit from trade as they specialize according to their advantage, but we must realize that *not all people within the country will benefit from trade*. Although the country as a whole becomes better off, there will be some gainers and some losers within the country. That is, the benefits of trade will not be distributed equally."

Analysis This passage from a textbook is a careful reminder to avoid the fallacy of composition in discussions of free trade.

4.2 Numbers

Numbers seem exact, but here we'll see how they can be very misleading.

Sometimes a sharp comparison using precise numbers is made, yet the comparison itself is nonsense.

Example 1   There were twice as many rapes as murders in our town.
   Analysis   This seems to say something important, but what? It's like saying that Dick has three apples and Zoe has four oranges, so who has more? More what?

Example 2   It's getting really violent in Las Vegas. There were 8% more murders this year than last.
   Analysis   This is a mistaken comparison. Las Vegas is growing rapidly and the number of tourists is growing, so it should be no surprise that the *number* of murders is going up, though the *rate* (how many murders per 100,000 population) might be going down. It's safer to live in a town of one million that had 20 murders last year than in a small town of 25,000 that had 6.

Citing numbers for rises or decreases can look precise, but you need to know where they started to be able to evaluate it. For example, Tom sees a stock for $60 and think it's a good deal. He buys it; a week later it's at $90, so he sells. He made $30—a 50% gain! His friend Wanda hears about it and buys the stock at $90; a week later it goes down to $60, so she panics and sells the stock. Wanda lost $30—a $33\frac{1}{3}$% loss. The same $30 is a different percentage depending on where you started.

$$50\%\uparrow \begin{bmatrix} \$90 \\ \$60 \end{bmatrix} \downarrow 33\tfrac{1}{3}\%$$

Or suppose a clothing store advertises a sale of sweaters at "25% off". You take that to mean 25% off the price they used to charge, which was $20, so you think you'll pay $15. But the store could mean 25% off the suggested retail price of $26, so it's now $19.50. You need to ask, "25% off *what*?"
   We call a comparison that makes something look impressive but the base of the comparison is not stated a *two times zero is still zero* comparison.

Example 3   Consolidated Computers reports a 32% increase in sales! Invest now!
   Analysis   This is a "two times zero is still zero" comparison. What were Consolidated Computers' sales last year? $500? $5,000? $500,000? $5,000,000? What that 32% represents matters in deciding whether to invest.

Often numbers are cited but there seems to be *no way the number could be known*.

Example 4   There were nearly 7.2 million people around the globe in 2000 who had at least $1 million in investable assets, an increase of 180,000 from 1999, said a study released Monday.
                                                   Albuquerque Tribune, May 15, 2001
   Analysis   How could they know? Who was looking in all those accounts? A survey? Who

did they ask? If you're worth a lot in Zimbabwe, do you want everyone to know? Or if your finances are in bad shape, you might want people to think you're rich. What are "investable assets"? Maybe the uncited report is a reliable survey, but what's said here is so vague and open to doubt as to how they could know it that we should ignore it as noise.

Mean, median, and mode of a collection of numbers

The *average* or *mean* of a collection of numbers is obtained by adding the numbers and then dividing by the number of items.

The *median* is the midway mark: the same number of items above as below.

The *mode* is the number most often attained.

Suppose we're given a collection of numbers 7, 9, 37, 22, 109, 9, 11. The *average* or *mean* is calculated as follows: Add $7 + 9 + 37 + 22 + 109 + 9 + 11 = 204$; dividing 204 by 7 we get 29.14, the average or mean. The *median* is 11. The *mode* is 9.

Or consider the marks students received on Dr. E's final exam:

score	number of students
95	3 students
94	7 students
92	1 student
90	4 students
75	1 student
62	4 students
57	5 students
55	4 students
52	2 students

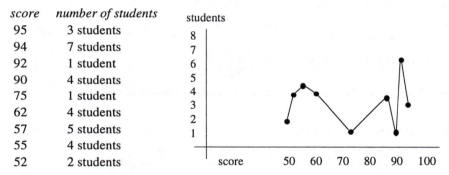

The grading scale was 90–100 = A, 80–89 = B, 70–79 = C, 60–69 = D, 59 and below = F. When Dr. E's department head asked him how the exam went, he told her, "Great! Just like you wanted, the average mark was 75%, a C." But she knows Dr. E too well, so she asks him, "What was the median score?" Again Dr. E can reply, "75." As many got above 75 as below 75. But knowing how clever Dr. E is with numbers, she asks him what the mode score was. Dr. E flushes, "Well, 94." Now she knows something is fishy. When she wanted the average score to be about 75, she was thinking of a graph that looked like this:

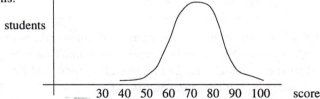

An average is a useful figure to know only if:

• There isn't too much variation in the figures.

• The average is pretty close to the median.

• The distribution is more or less bell-shaped.

4.3 Graphs

Graphs and tables are useful in making comparisons and correlations clearer.
But it's easy to be misled about what they say and where the numbers come from.

Example 1   Airlines with the highest ratio of reports of mishandled baggage in April

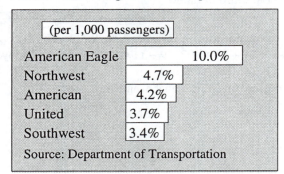

(per 1,000 passengers)	
American Eagle	10.0%
Northwest	4.7%
American	4.2%
United	3.7%
Southwest	3.4%
Source: Department of Transportation	

USA Today, June 13, 2002

Analysis   Which is it? Percentages (number per 100) or number per 1,000?

Example 2   "[The table] reveals the differences between whites and blacks in the United States
with respect to life expectancy, infant mortality, and maternal mortality.

INDICATOR	BLACK	WHITE	
Infant mortality rate, 1998	14.2	6.0	
Maternal mortality rate, 1997	20.8	5.8	

INDICATOR	BLACK MALES	BLACK FEMALES	WHITE MALES	WHITE FEMALES
Expected life at birth, 1998	66.1	74.2	73.8	79.6

Sources: Data from U.S. Department of Commerce, Bureau of the Census, *Statistical Abstract
of the United States*: *1999*; Bernard Guyer and Donna Hoyert, "Annual Summary of Vital
Statistics—1998," *Pediatrics* (December 1999); and Centers for Disease Control and
Prevention, *National Vital Statistics Report*, vol. 47, no. 19 (June 30, 1999)."

Analysis   The author cites good authorities, but a key piece of information is missing:
What do the numbers for infant mortality rate and maternal mortality rate refer to? Deaths per 100
live births? Deaths per 1,000 live births? Deaths per 10,000 live births? Deaths per 100 reported
pregnancies? . . . The significance of the comparison depends on this.

Example 3

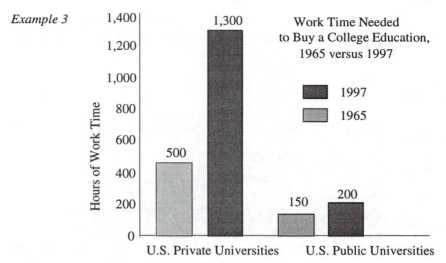

Work Time Needed
to Buy a College Education,
1965 versus 1997

Analysis This graph from an economics textbook looks clear, but personal experience should tell you it's wrong. The authors say the average hourly wage is about $13. So according to the graph the (average?) cost of a college education in 1997 at a U.S. public university was about $13/hour x 200 hours = $2600. But that wouldn't have been enough for even tuition and books for one year, much less housing and board, let alone for four years.

Example 4 "Wages in Japan and throughout northern Europe are similar. Indeed, workers in a number of other industrial countries receive higher compensation than American workers do, for the first time in many decades. According to the U.S. Bureau of Labor Statistics, in 1997 workers in U.S. manufacturing sectors made less than those in Germany, Belgium, the Netherlands, and Canada (see figure). However, U.S. compensation levels still remain well ahead of those in Japan, France, the United Kingdom, and many other countries."

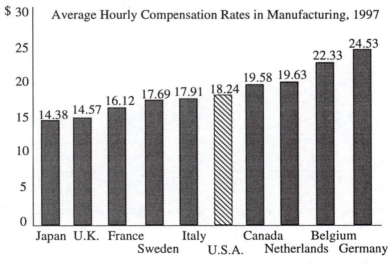

Analysis This passage combined with the graph looks impressive, but really it's an apples and oranges comparison. The passage first talks about hourly wages of all employees in the U.S. But the graph is only for workers in the manufacturing sector, which on the previous page of the text we're told accounts for about 18% of all civilian employment. Are the wages in the manufacturing sector higher or lower than the average in all sectors in any one country, in particular, the U.S.?

From a graph we can sometimes read off numbers as well as from a table. But graphs can distort comparisons. The next example shows that a graph can be misleading when either:

- *The baseline is not zero.*
- *The graph uses bars.*

Example 5

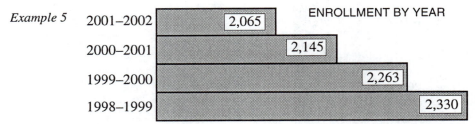

ENROLLMENT BY YEAR

2001–2002   2,065
2000–2001   2,145
1999–2000   2,263
1998–1999   2,330

Socorro, N.M. Consolidated Schools Accountability Report, 2000–2001

Analysis   The numbers here are correct, but the graph greatly exaggerates the differences between years. The enrollment in 2001– 2002 is 11.4% less than in 1998–1999, but the difference in the lengths of the bars representing those enrollments is 66%. Visually the difference appears even greater because we're comparing areas instead of comparing lengths.

Graphs can also create misleading comparisons by the choice of how *the measuring points on the axes are spaced.*

Example 6

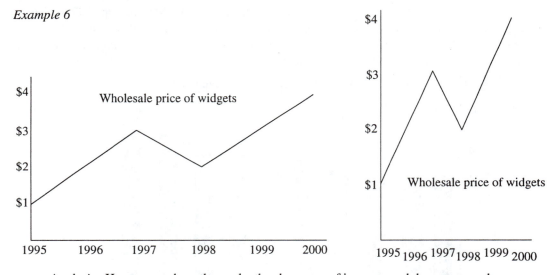

Analysis   Here we see how the angle, the sharpness of increase and decrease, can be exaggerated greatly by the spacing of the scales on the axes. This affects our perception of the volatility and the amount of increase or decrease of prices.

Here is another example in which the scales on the axes mislead.

Example 7

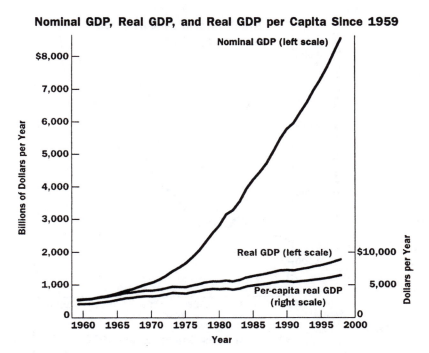

Nominal GDP, Real GDP, and Real GDP per Capita Since 1959

Analysis This graph from an economics text compares the growth in per-capita real GDP with growth in real GDP. But it creates a misleading visual comparison by combining different scales. The spacing on the scale on the right is completely arbitrary relative to the one on the left. And if $5,000 were two inches higher, it would seem that per-capita real GDP is growing much faster than real GDP, rather than vice versa.

Graphs can also distort statistics by the choice of *time period* that is presented.

Example 8 An economics text gives this graph and remarks that from 1966 to 1982 the prices of stocks were generally going down.

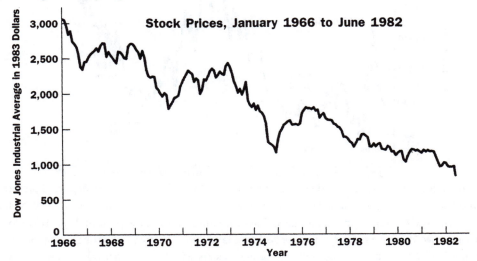

Stock Prices, January 1966 to June 1982

The text then presents the following graphs for two other time periods, noting in particular that from 1993 to 1998 stock prices were generally going up.

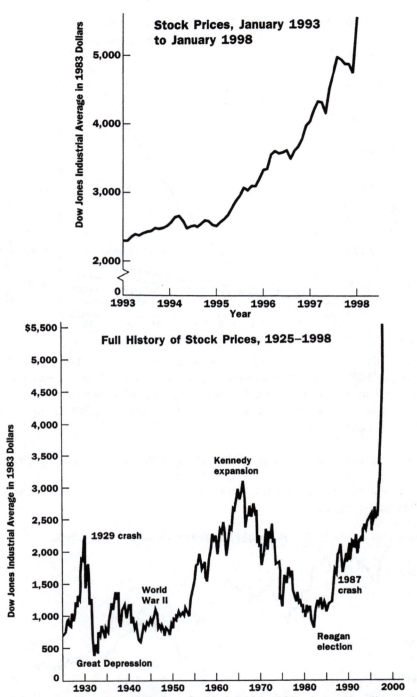

"A much longer and less-biased choice of period (1925–1998) gives a less distorted picture. It indicates that investments in stocks are sometimes profitable and sometimes unprofitable."

Analysis Why is the longer period apt for comparison to the present day? If we look at 1890 onwards, we'd have a different picture still (the label "Full History" is wrong). Maybe the best comparison for an analogy about investing in stocks is with the later periods because of new regulations on buying and selling stocks. These graphs, however, do compensate for inflation by stating the values in 1983 dollars—if they didn't, the comparisons would be worthless.

Example 9   Q: I am 47 years old. . . .   Could you please tell me how realistic is the notion of my average expenses increasing by 3 percent inflation rate a year, and will compounding it annually show me what my expected monthly expenses will be?

A: . . .   Three percent is actually the average annual inflation over the past century and is still higher than the average of 1.3 percent a year over the past two centuries. That said, some retirement planning programs suggest using 4 percent, since that is the average over the past 30 years. However, several decades is a small slice of American economic history and includes the high inflation years of the late 1970s and early 1980s.   Eric Tyson, *Albuquerque Journal*, August 26, 2002

Analysis   This is a much more thoughtful discussion of time periods in investing.

Sometimes a graph is an *implicit argument*.

Example 10

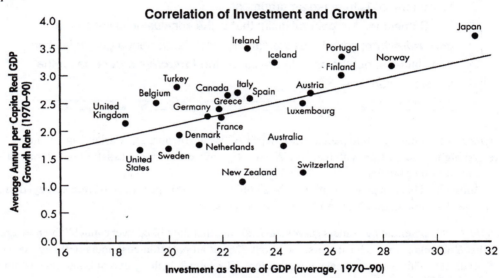

Analysis   By drawing the line in this graph, the author is asserting that investment and growth are correlated: both rise together. His premises are the data plotted as points. But the picture doesn't obviously support that. Why draw a line rather than a curve? And why this line? We can accept the correlation on the basis of this graph only if we take it as an appeal to the author's authority.

Sometimes a diagram looks like a graph, but *it's only an illustration*.

Example 11   [From an economics text] The maximum willingness to pay of a given person is often called his or her *reservation price*. . . .

Demand curve for apartments with many demanders.

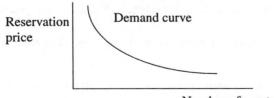

Analysis   A graph is a visual display of quantitative information. This diagram isn't a graph relating quantities that are actually measured. It's an illustration to help us "see" a theory.

4.4 Generalizing

In this section we'll learn how to generalize from our experience
and how to evaluate generalizations that others make.

> **Generalizing** To *generalize* is to conclude a claim about a group,
> the **population**, from a claim about some part of it, the **sample**.
> To generalize is to make an argument.
>   Sometimes the general claim that is the conclusion is called the
> **generalization**; sometimes we call the whole argument a generalization.
> The claims about the sample are called the **inductive evidence** for the
> generalization.

Example 1 In a study of 5,000 people who owned ATVs in Anchorage, Alaska, Riga owners
expressed higher satisfaction with their ATVs. So Riga owners are more satisfied with their ATVs
than owners of other brands.
    Analysis This is a generalization. The sample is the 5,000 people who were surveyed in
Anchorage. The population is all ATV owners everywhere.

Example 2 Of potential customers surveyed, 72% said that they liked "very much" the new green
color that Yoda plans to use for its cars. So about 72% of all potential customers will like that color.
    Analysis This is a statistical generalization. The sample is the group of potential customers
interviewed. The population is all potential customers.

Example 3 Every time the minimum wage is raised, there's squawking that it will cause inflation
and decrease employment. And every time it doesn't. So watch for the same bad arguments again
this time.
    Analysis The unstated conclusion is that raising the minimum wage will neither cause
inflation nor decrease employment. This is a generalization from the past to the future. The sample is
all times in the past that the minimum wage was raised. The population is all times it was raised or
will be raised.

Example 4 The doctor tells you to fast from 10 p.m. At 10 a.m. she gives you glucose to drink.
Forty-five minutes later she takes some of your blood and has it analyzed. She concludes you don't
have diabetes.
    Analysis This is a generalization. The sample is the blood the doctor took. The population is
all the blood you have in your body.

Example 5 Wanda goes to the city council meeting with a petition signed by all the people who live
on her block requesting that a street light be put in. Addressing the city council, she says, "Everyone
on this block wants a street light here."

Analysis This is not a generalization. There's no argument from some to more, since the sample equals the population.

What conditions should a sample satisfy for a generalization to be good?

> **Representative sample** A sample is representative if no one subgroup of the whole population is represented more than its proportion in the population. A sample is **biased** if it is not representative.

For a generalization to be good we should have a representative sample. But how can we get one? Lots of people think it's good enough to do **haphazard sampling**: *choose the sample with no intentional bias.* But haphazard sampling is unreliable. For example, to determine the attitudes of students about the cost of tuition, Tom gave a questionnaire to the first 20 students he met coming out of the student union. He was choosing his sample haphazardly. That sample may be representative, but there's no reason to believe so. Those students might be coming from a meeting of the student MBA association, or the Green party, or . . . . Advised of the problem, Tom enlisted three of his friends to give the questionnaire to the first 20 students they meet coming out of the student union, the administration offices, and the largest classroom building at 9 a.m., 1 p.m., and 6 p.m. But there's no reason to think that new sample is representative either—all the players on intercollegiate sports teams might be gone for the day. What's needed is to choose a sample by a method called "random sampling".

> **Random sampling** A sample is chosen **randomly** if at every choice there is an equal chance for any of the remaining members of the population to be picked.

Suppose Tom assigns a number to each student, writes the numbers on slips of paper, puts them in a fishbowl, and draws one number at a time. That looks like a random selection. But there's a chance that slips with longer numbers will have more ink and fall to the bottom of the bowl when he shakes it. Or the slips might not all be the same size. So to get a *random selection* we usually use tables of random numbers prepared by mathematicians. Most spreadsheet programs for home computers can generate tables of random numbers. For Tom's survey he could get a list of all students; if the first number on the table is 413, he'd pick the 413th student on the list; if the second number is 711, he'd pick the 711th student on the list; and so on until he has a big enough sample.

Suppose that at Tom's school there are 20,000 students, of which 250 are MBA students, and Tom picks a sample *randomly*. Then the chance that *one* student picked at random would be an MBA student is $250/20{,}000 = 1/80$. If his sample is 300 students, the chance that half of them would be MBA students is very, very small. It is very likely, however, that 3 or 4 of them (1/80 of 300) will be MBA students.

On the other hand, suppose roughly 50% of the students at the school are female.

Then each time a student is chosen at random there's about a 50% chance it will be a female. So in a random sample of 300 students the chance is very high that the sample will have close to 50% females.

The ***law of large numbers*** says, roughly, that if the probability of something occurring is X percent, then over the long run the percentage of times that happens will be about X percent. For example, the chance of a flip of a fair coin landing heads is 50%. So although you may get a run of 8 tails, then 5 heads, then 4 tails, then 36 heads to start, in the long run, repeating the flipping, *eventually* the number of heads will tend toward 50%. However, that "eventually" may be a long time in the future.

Example 6   Dick (at the roulette table): It's come up red 12 times in a row. I'll bet on black— it's bound to come up black several times in a row now.

Analysis   Wrong. For example, if the spins could come up red 100 times in a row, black could come up as often as red by coming up just one more time than red every 100 spins for the next 10,000 spins. Each spin of the roulette wheel is independent of all others.

> **The gambler's fallacy**   The gambler's fallacy is to reason that a run of events of a certain kind makes a run of contrary events more likely in order to even up the probabilities.

If you choose a large sample randomly, the chance is very high that it will be representative. That's because the chance of any one subgroup being over-represented is small—not nonexistent, but small. It doesn't matter if you know anything about the composition of the population in advance. After all, to know how many MBA students there are, how many married women, how many men, . . . , you'd need to know almost everything about the population in advance. And that's what we use surveys to find out.

With a random sample we have good reason to believe the sample is representative. A sample chosen haphazardly *might* give a representative sample, but we have no good reason to believe it does.

Weak argument	Strong argument
Sample is chosen *haphazardly*.	Sample is chosen *randomly*.
Therefore, the sample is representative.	Therefore, the sample is representative.
Lots of ways the sample could be biased.	Low probability the sample could be biased.

The classic example that haphazard sampling can be bad, even with an enormous sample, is the poll done in 1936 by *Literary Digest*. The magazine mailed out 10,000,000 ballots asking people who they would vote for in the 1936 presidential election. The magazine received back 2,300,000 ballots. With that huge sample, the magazine confidently predicted that Alf Landon would win. Roosevelt received 60% of the vote, one of the biggest wins ever. What went wrong? The magazine selected its sample from lists of its own subscribers and telephone and automobile owners. In 1936 that sample was the wealthy class, which preferred Alf Landon.

We need a representative sample for a good generalization. But that's not enough. We also need that our sample is big enough.

> **Sample size** For a generalization to be good, the sample has to be big enough. Generalizing from a sample that is obviously too small is called a **hasty generalization** based on **anecdotal evidence**.

Example 7 Both MBA graduates I met have got high-paying jobs, so I'm going to get an MBA.

Analysis The speaker is assuming the generalization that (almost) all MBA graduates get high-paying jobs. But that's just a hasty generalization from his experience.

How big does a sample have to be? Roughly, the idea is to measure how much more likely it is that your generalization is going to be accurate as you increase the number in your sample. If you want to find out how many people in your class of 300 economics students are spending 10 hours a week on the homework, you might ask 15 or 20. If you interview 30 you might get a better picture, but there's a limit. After you've asked 100, you probably won't get a much different result if you ask 150. And if you've asked 200, do you really think your generalization will be different if you ask 250?

Often you can rely on common sense when small numbers are involved. But when we generalize to a very large population, say 2,500, or 25,000, or 250,000,000, how big the sample should be cannot be explained without at least a mini-course on statistics. In evaluating statistical generalizations, you have to expect that the people doing the sampling have looked at enough examples, which is reasonable if it's a respected organization, a well-known polling company, physicians, or a drug company that has to answer to the Food and Drug Administration. Surprisingly, perhaps, 1,500 is typically adequate for the sample size when surveying all adults in the U.S.

How big the sample needs to be also depends on how much *variation* there is in the population regarding the aspect you're investigating. If there is very little variation, then a small sample chosen haphazardly will do. Lots of variation (or where you don't know how much variation there is) demands a very large sample, and random sampling is the best way to get a representative one.

Example 8 It's incredible how much information they can put on a CD. I just bought one that contains a whole encyclopedia.

Analysis This is a good generalization. The unstated conclusion is that every CD can contain as much information as this one that has the encyclopedia on it. There is little variation in the production of CDs for computers, so a sample of one is sufficient.

There's one more condition a sample must satisfy for a generalization to be good.

> **The sample is studied well** The sample has to be studied well for a generalization to be good.

For example, the doctor taking your blood to see if you have diabetes won't get a reliable result if her test tube isn't clean or if she forgets to tell you to fast the night before. You won't find out the real attitudes of students about tuition if you ask a biased question. Picking a random sample of bolts won't help you determine whether the bolts are O.K. if all you do is inspect them visually, not with a microscope or a stress test.

Questionnaires and surveys are particularly problematic. Questions need to be formulated without bias. Even then, you have to rely on the respondents answering truthfully. For example, surveys on sexual habits are notorious for inaccurate reporting: Invariably the number of times that women in the U.S. report they engaged in sexual intercourse with a man in the last week, or month, or year, is much lower than the reports that men give of sexual intercourse with a woman during that time. The figures are so different that it would be impossible for both groups to be answering accurately.

In summary, then, we have the following conditions for a generalization to be good.

Premises needed for a good generalization

- The sample is representative.

- The sample is big enough.

- The sample is studied well.

Still, it's never reasonable to believe a statistical generalization whose conclusion is exactly precise.

Example 9 In a survey, 37% of the people in Socorro who were interviewed said they wear glasses, so 37% of all people in Socorro wear glasses.

Analysis No matter how many people in Socorro are surveyed, short of virtually all of them, we can't be confident that exactly 37% of all people in the town wear glasses. Rather, "37%, more or less, wear glasses" is the right conclusion.

That "more or less" can be made fairly precise according to a theory of statistics. The ***margin of error*** gives the range in which the actual number for that population is likely to fall. The ***confidence level*** measures the strength of the argument for the statistical conclusion, given the survey method and responses as premises.

Example 10 The opinion poll says that when voters were asked their preference, the incumbent was favored by 53% and the challenger by 47%, with a margin of error of 2% and a confidence level of 95%. So the incumbent will win tomorrow.

Analysis From this survey they are concluding that the percentage of *all* voters who favor the incumbent is between 51% and 55%, while the challenger is favored by between 45% and 49%. That the confidence level is 95% means that there is a 95% chance it's true that the actual percentage of voters who prefer the incumbent is between 51% and 55%. If the confidence level were 70%, then the survey wouldn't be very reliable: There would be a 3-out-of-10 chance the conclusion is false. Typically, if the confidence level is below 95%, results won't be announced.

The bigger the sample, the higher the confidence level and the lower the margin of error. The problem always is to decide how much it's worth in extra time and expense to increase the sample size in order to get a stronger argument. For example, with a shipment of 30 insulating tiles, inspecting 3 and finding them O.K. would normally allow you to conclude that all the tiles are O.K. But if they're for the space shuttle, where a bad tile could doom the spacecraft, you'd want to inspect each and every one of them.

> **Risk** Risk doesn't change how strong an argument you have, only how strong an argument you want before you'll accept the conclusion.

One mistake which we all make sooner or later is to pay *selective attention*: We note only what's unusual. It seems that buttered toast always lands buttered side down, because you notice it when it does.

Here is a range of examples that you can work through to begin to master how to evaluate and make generalizations.

Example 11 Every time I've seen a stranger come to Dick's gate, Spot has barked. So Spot will always bark at strangers at Dick's gate.

Analysis This is a bad generalization: The sample is chosen haphazardly. There's no reason to believe it's representative.

Example 12 In a study of 5,000 people who owned ATVs in Anchorage, Alaska, Riga owners expressed higher satisfaction with their ATVs. So Riga owners are more satisfied with their ATVs than owners of other brands.

Analysis This is a bad generalization: The sample is not representative. At best the evidence could lead to a conclusion about all ATV owners in Anchorage, Alaska.

Example 13 Maria has asked all but three of the thirty-six people in her class whether they've ever lied on their taxes. Only two said "yes." So Maria concludes that almost no one in the class has lied.

Analysis This is a bad generalization. The sample is big enough and may be representative, but it's not studied well. People are not likely to admit to a stranger that they've lied on their taxes; an anonymous questionnaire is needed.

Example 14 People who invest with the brokerage Spring-Up get terrific returns on their money. I know, because my grandfather has had an account with them since 1950 and he's averaged over 12%!

Analysis This is bad, a hasty generalization.

Example 15 Dick: A study I read said people with large hands make more on the stock market.

Lee: I guess that's why I lost a bundle last year.

Analysis This is a bad application of a generalization. Perhaps the study was done carefully with a random sample. But you don't need a study to know that people with large hands make more on the stock market: Eight-year-olds have smaller hands, and they invest very badly. *All people* is the wrong population to study.

Example 16 Of chimpanzees fed one pound of chocolate per day in addition to their usual diet, 72% became obese within two months. Therefore, it is likely that most humans who eat 1% or more of their body weight in chocolate daily will become obese within two months.

Analysis A generalization is needed to make this analogy good: 72% of *all* chimpanzees, more or less, will become obese if fed one pound of chocolate per day in addition to their usual diet. Whether this is a good generalization will depend on whether the researchers can claim that their sample is representative. The analogy then needs claims about the similarity of chimpanzee physiology to human physiology, the weight of chimpanzees, and their activity level.

Example 17 Lee: Every rich person I've met invested heavily in the stock market. So I'll invest in the stock market, too.

Analysis This is a confused attempt to generalize. Perhaps Lee thinks that the evidence he cites gives the conclusion that if you invest in the stock market, you'll get rich(er). But that's arguing backwards, confusing (1) "If you invest in the stock market, you'll get rich" with (2) "If you're rich, then you will have invested in the stock market." The population for (1) is all investors in the stock market, not just the rich ones. It's a case of selective attention.

Example 18 When the price of a good goes up, there will be fewer people who will buy it.

Analysis As one economics text says, "Economics, like the other social sciences, is concerned with reaching generalizations about human behavior."

Example 19 People in New Mexico are very independent and almost always prefer to live in separate homes rather than apartments. So we should allow for more subdivisions to be built in Albuquerque.

Analysis If we drop the vague phrase "are very independent", the premise here is a general claim that we shouldn't accept *without a good generalization establishing it*. The conclusion of the argument is a normative claim that requires some normative premise, too.

Example 20 Experience, however, shows that the fancied or real insecurity of capital, when not under the immediate control of its owner, together with the natural disinclination which every man has to quit the country of his birth and connections, and intrust himself, with all his habits fixed, to a strange government and new laws, check the emigration of capital. These feelings, which I should be sorry to see weakened, induce most men of property to be satisfied with a low rate of profits in their own country, rather than seek a more advantageous employment for their wealth in foreign nations.

David Ricardo, *Principles of Political Economy and Taxation*

Analysis The appeal to "experience" here is an example of how generalizing was done before the methods of analysis given in this chapter became commonplace in the twentieth century.

Example 21 "According to the National Pork Producers Council (www.nppc.org), average hog market weight is 250 pounds, and it takes about 3.5 pounds of feed to produce one pound of live hog weight."

Analysis It's a good appeal to authority to accept this generalization given by the National Pork Producers Council. Though we don't have access to the data they used nor how they interpreted it, they are a big enough organization to employ good statisticians, and they have no reason to lie to their own members.

Example 22 "[1] A worker with a particularly good job has a stronger incentive to keep it than a worker who could easily find a similar job at another firm. [2] A worker with a strong incentive to keep a job is likely to do high-quality work and maintain high productivity. [3] By paying unusually high wages, firms can give employees incentives for good performance. In this way, [4] high wages can substitute to some extent for active supervision of workers, reducing a firm's management costs.

When Henry Ford started the Ford Motor Company, he encountered a very high quit rate among his employees. (Also, he frequently fired workers.) The company's employee turnover was

370 percent in 1913; Ford had to hire 370 people each year just to keep 100 jobs filled. On an average day, more than 10 percent of workers failed to show up for their shifts. Despite worker unhappiness, Ford could choose among long lines of people who wanted to work there, so it could easily hire new workers. Nevertheless, the company decided in January 1914 to double its wage from $2.50 to $5.00 per hour (in today's dollars). The $2.50 wage was an equilibrium wage. (If it had been below equilibrium, Ford would not have easily found new employees to hire.) Setting the wage above the equilibrium level, however, reduced the quit rate by 87 percent, and absenteeism fell 75 percent. Workers improved their performance, and firings fell 90 percent."

Analysis   In this passage from an economics text, [1] and [2] are generalizations about human behavior, which are meant to lead to [3] and [4].

But why should we believe [1] and [2]? The story of Ford Motor Company's experience is illustrative, meant to make the claims more memorable. But it's only anecdotal evidence. You might think that the claims are obvious, since they reflect what you reckon you would do, but that's just anecdotal evidence, too. As in many textbooks, the only reason given to believe these claims (which is implicit) is the authority of the author.

4.5 Cause and Effect

In this section we'll learn how to recognize and evaluate claims about cause and effect, which are at the heart of economics.

Example 1   Here are some section headings from a couple of economics texts:
- The Price Elasticity in Demand and its Determinants
- How Price Ceilings Affect Market Outcomes
- How a Higher Price Raises Producer Surplus
- The Effects of an Import Quota
- Why Private Solutions Do Not Always Work
- What Causes the Labor Demand to Shift?
- The Influence of Monetary and Fiscal Policy on Aggregate Demand
- The Cost of Reducing Inflation
- What Makes Economies Grow?
- How to Increase Employment
- How Ongoing Inflation Arises

Analysis   All these are about cause and effect: determinant = cause; raises = causes an increase; work = effectively cause; influence = partial cause; cost = unwanted effects; makes = causes; how to = a recipe for causing; arises = comes as an effect.

But what exactly is a cause? Consider what Dick said early this morning about his dog Spot:

Spot caused me to wake up.

Spot is the thing that somehow caused Dick to wake up. But it's not just that Spot existed. It's what he was doing that caused Dick to wake up: "Spot's barking caused Dick to wake up." So Spot's barking is the cause? What kind of thing is barking? The easiest way to describe the cause is to say, "Spot barked." The easiest way to describe the effect is to say, "Dick woke up." *Causes and effects can be described with claims.*

> **Causal claims**   A causal claim is a claim that can be rewritten as "X causes (caused) Y."   A ***particular*** causal claim is one in which a single claim can describe the (purported) cause and a single claim can describe the (purported) effect. A ***general*** causal claim is a causal claim that generalizes many particular causal claims.

"Spot's barking caused Dick to wake up" is a particular causal claim. The purported cause can be described with a single claim, "Spot was barking." The purported effect can be described with a single claim, "Dick woke up." We could generalize from this particular cause and effect, for example, "Very loud barking by a dog near someone who is sleeping *causes* him or her to wake up, if he or she is not deaf." For that to be true, lots of particular causal claims must be true.

Since causes and effects can be described with claims, we can use all we know about claims in the analysis of cause and effect, for instance, whether they are objective or subjective, and whether a sentence is too vague to describe a cause or effect.

Example 2 The police car's siren got me to pull over.
    Analysis This is a particular causal claim. The purported cause is (can be described as) "The police car had its siren going." The purported effect is "I pulled over."

Example 3 Because Suzy was late, Tom missed the beginning of the movie.
    Analysis This is a particular causal claim. The purported cause is (can be described as) "Suzy was late." The purported effect is "Tom missed the beginning of the movie."

Example 4 The rise in interest rates in October caused a drop in home sales in December compared to November, and also compared to December one year ago.
    Analysis This is a particular causal claim. The purported cause is "Interest rates rose in October." The purported effect is "There was a drop in home sales in December compared to November, and also compared to December one year ago."

Example 5 Rising interest rates cause home sales to drop.
    Analysis This is too vague to count as a claim, so it's certainly not a causal claim.

Example 6 In the United States, interest rates going up 20% above what they were in the previous month causes home sales to drop by 5% in no more than 3 months' time compared to the month previous to that one and compared to one year earlier.
    Analysis This is a general causal claim. For it to be true, lots of particular causal claims have to be true.

Example 7 Unemployment rising above 7% makes consumers less willing to spend money.
    Analysis This is a general causal claim asserting subjective effects. To establish the purported effect, an objective test is often invoked: the consumer confidence index is lower. That is indeed objective, for it measures responses people give to questions on a survey.

Example 8 In any month when unemployment first rises above 7%, American consumers will spend 3% less on household appliances in the following month.
    Analysis This is a general causal claim asserting objective effects.

Example 9 Lack of rain caused the crops to fail.
    Analysis The purported cause here is "There was no rain", and the purported effect is "The crops failed." This example was true a few years ago in the Midwest. Causes need not be something active; almost any claim that describes the world could qualify as a cause.

We'll look now at what conditions are needed for a causal claim to be true.

1. The cause and effect both happened.

That is, the claims describing the cause and the effect are both true. For example, we don't say that Spot's barking caused Dick to wake up if either Dick didn't wake up or Spot didn't bark.

2. It's (nearly) impossible for the cause to happen and the effect not to happen.

That is, it has to be (nearly) impossible for the claim describing the cause to be true and the claim describing the effect to be false. For example, it can't be just a coincidence that Spot barked and Dick woke up for us to say that Spot's barking caused Dick to wake up.

This second condition is exactly the relation of premises to conclusion in a valid or strong argument. But here we're not trying to convince anyone that the conclusion is true: We know that Dick woke up. What we can carry over from our study of arguments is how to look for all the possibilities—all the ways the premises could be true and the conclusion false—to determine if there is cause and effect. And just as with arguments, we will often need to supply unstated premises to show that the effect follows from the cause.

For example, a lot has to be true for it to be impossible for "Spot barked" to be true and "Dick woke up" to be false: Dick was sleeping soundly up to the time that Spot barked; Spot barked at 3 a.m.; Spot was close to where Dick was sleeping; . . . . We could go on forever. But as with arguments, we state what we think is important and leave out the obvious. If someone challenged us, we could add, "There was no earthquake at the time" —but we just assume that.

> **Normal conditions** The obvious and plausible unstated claims that are needed to establish that the relation between purported cause and purported effect is valid or strong are called the normal conditions for the causal claim.

For a general causal claim, such as "Very loud barking by a dog near someone who is sleeping *causes* him or her to wake up, if he or she is not deaf", the normal conditions won't be specific to just the one time Spot woke Dick, but will be general.

3. The cause precedes the effect.

The claim describing the cause becomes true before the claim describing the effect is true.

For example, we don't accept that Spot's barking caused Dick to wake up if Spot began barking only after Dick woke up. The cause has to precede the effect: "Spot barked" became true before "Dick woke up" became true.

4. The cause makes a difference.

If there were no cause, then there would be no effect.

Dr. E has a desperate fear of elephants. So he buys a special wind chime and puts it outside his door to keep the elephants away. He lives in Socorro, New Mexico, at 4,500 feet above sea level in a desert, and he confidently claims that the wind chime causes the elephants to stay away. After all, ever since he put up the wind chime he hasn't seen any elephants.

Why are we sure the wind chime being up did not cause elephants to stay away? Because even if there had been no wind chime, the elephants would have stayed away. Which elephants? All elephants. The wind chime works, but so would anything else. The wind chime doesn't make a difference.

5. There is no common cause.

We don't say that night causes day, because there is a common cause of both "It was night" and "It is now day," namely, "The earth is rotating relative to the sun."

If Dick asserts that Zoe is irritable because she can't sleep properly, and Tom responds by saying that she's both irritable and can't sleep because she's been drinking four cups of espresso every afternoon, then Tom has suggested a common cause that throws doubt on Dick's causal claim.

Now we can sum up the conditions needed for a causal claim to be true.

Necessary conditions for cause and effect

1. The cause and effect happened (are true).

2. It is (nearly) impossible for the cause to happen (be true) and the effect not to happen (be false), given the normal conditions.

3. The cause precedes the effect.

4. The cause makes a difference—if the cause had not happened, the effect would not have happened, given the normal conditions.

5. There is no common cause.

Common mistakes in reasoning about cause and effect

A. Tracing the cause too far back

It's sometimes said that the cause must be close in space and time to the effect. But the astronomer is right when she says that a star shining caused the image on the photograph, even though that star is very far away and the light took millions of years to arrive. The problem isn't how distant in time and space the cause is from the effect. The problem is how much has come between the cause and effect—whether we can specify the normal conditions. *When we trace a cause too far back, the problem is that the normal conditions begin to multiply.* There are too many conditions for us to imagine what would be necessary to establish that it is impossible for the cause to have been true and the effect false. When you get that far back, you know you've gone too far.

Example 10 Peter: I missed class the day they covered opportunity cost. That's why I became a book editor instead of an investment banker.

Analysis This is tracing the cause too far back to be able to state the normal conditions.

B. Confusing cause with effect

If reversing cause and effect sounds just as plausible as the original claim, we should investigate the evidence further before making a judgment.

Example 11 Suzy: Sitting too close to the TV ruins your eyesight.
   Zoe: How do you know?
   Suzy: Well, two of my grade school friends used to sit really close to the TV, and
           both of them wear really thick glasses now.

Zoe: Maybe they sat so close because they had bad eyesight.

Analysis Zoe hasn't shown that Suzy's claim is false. But her suggestion that cause and effect have been reversed raises sufficient doubt not to accept it without more evidence.

C. *Looking too hard for a cause*

We look for causes because we want to understand, so we can control our future. But sometimes the best we can say is that it's *coincidence*.

Before your jaw drops open in amazement when a friend tells you a piano fell on his teacher the day after your friend dreamt that she saw him in a recital, remember the law of large numbers: If it's possible, given long enough, it'll happen. After all, most of us dream —say one dream a night for fifty million adults in the U.S. That's three hundred and fifty million dreams per week. With the elasticity in interpreting dreams and what counts as a "dream coming true", it would be amazing if a lot of dreams *didn't* "accurately predict the future".

But doesn't everything have a cause? Shouldn't we look for it? For some things that happen in our lives we won't be able to figure out the cause—we just don't know enough. We must, normally, ascribe some happenings to chance, to coincidence, or else we'll have paranoia and end up paying a lot of money to phone psychics.

> ***Post hoc ergo propter hoc*** ("after this, therefore because of this")
> is the fallacy of claiming that there is cause and effect just because
> one claim became true after another.

Example 12 I scored well on that last exam and I was wearing my red plaid shirt. I better wear it every time I take an exam.

Analysis This is just *post hoc* reasoning.

Example 13 A recent study showed that everyone who uses heroin started with marijuana. So smoking marijuana causes heroin use.

Analysis And they all probably drank milk first, too. Without further evidence, this is just *post hoc ergo propter hoc*.

We'll go through all the steps in evaluating a causal claim in the next example.

Example 14

The cat made Spot run away.

Analysis

Cause: What is the cause? It's not just that a cat existed. Perhaps the cause is "A cat meowed close to Spot."

Effect: Spot ran away.

Cause and effect true: The effect is clearly true. The cause is highly plausible: Almost all things that meow (where people are walking dogs) are cats.

Cause precedes effect: Yes.

It is (nearly) impossible for the cause to be true and the effect false: This is not clear. We have to establish the normal conditions. Spot normally chases cats, given the opportunity. But what is "given the opportunity"? We have no reason to believe he'll chase just any cat anywhere at any time at any distance from him. We do not know those normal conditions. At best we can say that it's highly unlikely in this situation that the cat could meow and Spot not chase it.

The cause makes a difference: Would Spot have run away even if the cat had not meowed near him? It would seem that under the normal conditions of a walk with Dick he wouldn't, since Dick is holding the leash loosely, not prepared for Spot to run away at any moment. But would Spot have chased the cat even if it had not meowed? Perhaps yes, if he had been aware of it.

So let's revise the cause to "A cat meowed close to Spot, and he heard it." Now we can reasonably believe that the cause made a difference.

Is there a common cause? Perhaps the cat was hit by a meat truck and lots of meat fell out, and Spot ran away for that? No, Spot wouldn't have barked. Nor would he have growled. Perhaps the cat is a hapless bystander in a fight between dogs, one of whom is Spot's friend. We do not know if this is the case. So it is possible that there is a common cause, but it seems very unlikely.

In the end we have good reason to believe the original claim on the revised interpretation that the cause is "A cat meowed close to Spot, and he heard it."

The steps in the last example are the ones we should go through in establishing a causal claim. If we can show that one of them fails, however, there's no need to check all the others.

The best way to avoid making common mistakes in reasoning about causes is to *experiment*. Conjecture possible causes, then by experiment eliminate them until there is only one. Check that one: Does it make a difference? If the purported cause is eliminated, is there still the effect? Often we can't do an experiment, but we can do an imaginary experiment. That's what we've always done in checking for validity: **Imagine the possibilities**.

Here are some examples to help you work through these ideas.

Example 15 The President's speech on farm issues made the price of corn rise 17% the next day.

Analysis The purported cause is "The President gave a speech on farm issues", and the purported effect is "The price of corn rose 17% the next day". Did the purported cause make a difference? A few hours after the President's speech, crop reports were released that showed the corn harvest would be down 13% due to drought. Those reports alone would have been enough to ensure higher corn prices. We have no reason to believe that the President's speech was the cause.

Example 16 Rudolfo's greed made him lie about the financial condition of the company.

Analysis The purported cause here is subjective: "Rudolfo was greedy." But that wouldn't have been enough to ensure the effect. It was crucial that he was asked advice by one of his investing clients who wasn't likely to check up, and Rudolfo's firm held stock in the company he was recommending so he would receive a big commission for selling the stock, and he knew that the company was likely to go bankrupt in the next six months. These hardly seem like normal conditions, so perhaps "Rudolfo was greedy" is only one of several claims that we can say are jointly the cause: We need to give a fuller description of the world.

Example 17   Money causes counterfeiting.

Analysis   This is a general causal claim covering every particular claim like "That there was money in this society caused this person to counterfeit the currency." We certainly have lots of inductive evidence. The problem seems to be that though this is true, it's uninteresting. It's tracing the cause too far back. There being money in a society is part of the normal conditions when we have the effect that someone counterfeited currency.

Example 18   "When more and more people are thrown out of work, unemployment results."
President Calvin Coolidge

Analysis   This isn't cause and effect; it's a definition.

Example 19   Maria: Fear of getting fired causes me to get to work on time.

Analysis   It seems that fear is the cause here. But what is fear? We can describe the purported cause as "Maria is afraid of getting fired" and the effect as "Maria gets to work on time."

Is it possible for Maria to be afraid of getting fired and still not get to work on time? Certainly, but not, perhaps, under normal conditions: Maria sets her alarm; the electricity doesn't go off; there isn't bad weather; Maria doesn't oversleep; . . .

But doesn't the causal claim mean it's because she's afraid that Maria makes sure that these conditions will be true, or that she'll get to work even if one or more is false? She doesn't let herself oversleep due to her fear. In that case how can we judge whether what Maria said is true? It's easy to think of cases where the cause is true and the effect false. So we have to add normal conditions. But that Maria gets to work regardless of conditions that aren't normal is what makes her consider her fear to be the cause.

Subjective causes are often a matter of feeling, some sense that we control what we do. They are often too vague for us to classify as true or false.

Example 20   Dick: Hold the steering wheel.
Zoe: What are you doing? Stop! Are you crazy?
Dick: I'm just taking my sweater off.
Zoe: I can't believe you did that. It's *so* dangerous.
Dick: Don't be silly. I've done it a thousand times before.
         Crash . . . Later . . .
Dick: You had to turn the steering wheel!? That made us crash.

Analysis   The purported cause is that Zoe turned the steering wheel. The effect is that the car crashed. The necessary criteria are satisfied. But Zoe's turning the steering wheel is a *foreseeable consequence* of Dick making her take the wheel, which is the real cause. The normal conditions are not just what has to be true before the cause, but sometimes also what will normally *follow* the cause.

Example 21   Dick: Wasn't that awful what happened to old Mr. Grzegorczyk?
Zoe: You mean those tree trimmers who dropped a huge branch on him and killed him?
Dick: You only got half the story. He had a heart attack in his car and pulled over to the side.
         He was lying on the pavement when the branch hit him and would've died anyway.

Analysis   What's the cause of Mr. Grzegorczyk dying? It seems that the tree branch falling on him didn't make a difference, since he would have died anyway. But the tree branch falling on him isn't a *foreseeable consequence*, part of the normal conditions of his stumbling out of his car with a heart attack. It's an *intervening cause*.

Example 22   Tom: The only time I've had a really bad backache is right after I went bicycling early in the morning when it was so cold last week. Bicycling never bothered me before. So it must be the cold weather that caused my back to hurt after cycling.

   Analysis   Cause: It was cold when Tom went cycling. Effect: Tom got a backache. The criteria seem to be satisfied. But Tom might have overlooked another cause. He also had an upset stomach, so maybe it was the flu. Or maybe it was tension, since he'd had a fight with Suzy the night before. He'll have to try cycling in the cold again to find out. Even then he may be looking too hard for *the* cause, when it may be only *a* cause. Another possibility: Tom will never know for sure.

   When several claims together are taken *jointly* as the cause, we say that each is (describes) *a cause* or that each is a ***causal factor***.

Example 23   The Treaty of Versailles caused hyperinflation in Germany in the 1920s.

   Analysis   The purported cause must be something like "The Treaty of Versailles was agreed to and enforced." The effect is "There was hyperinflation in Germany in the 1920s." To analyze a conjecture like this, an historian will write a book. The normal conditions have to be spelled out. It has to be shown that it was a foreseeable consequence of the enforcement of the Treaty of Versailles that there would be hyperinflation. But was it foreseeable that France would take over German industry in the Ruhr? More plausible is that the signing of the Treaty of Versailles was *a* cause, not *the* cause of hyperinflation; that is, it was one of many factors that caused hyperinflation to occur.

Example 24   Sunspots cause stock prices to rise.

   Analysis   Suppose your finance teacher tells you this general causal claim, and she backs it up with data showing a very good correlation between the appearance of large sunspots and rises in the Dow Jones index. But a correlation, though needed for a general causal claim, doesn't establish cause and effect by itself. It's hard to imagine a common cause, but coincidence can't be ruled out. If we look around the world long enough, we'll eventually find *some* phenomenon that can be correlated to the rise and fall in stock prices. Even if there were a very exact correlation between the size of the sunspots and the percentage of increase in the Dow Jones average two days later, we still want a theory—normal conditions that give us a way to trace how the sunspots cause the price rises. That is, we want an explanation, the nature of which we'll study in Section 5.1.

Example 25   Christopher Jenck's first essay on immigration, "Who Should Get In?" [November 29, 2001] has many virtues, including erudition, range, and grace, but also a subtle flaw. This lies in the unexamined premise that the *immigrants* themselves are the causal agents. According to this premise, illiterate, low-skilled, and otherwise disadvantaged persons first, somehow, *arrive*. They *then* bid down the wage rates for less-skilled occupations. And, if successful, *they displace* native workers who had previously held those jobs but who reject them once wages fall.

   Quantity is cause, price is effect. This is the famous mechanism of supply and demand, which economists love. It leads directly to a policy focus on permissible quantities of unskilled labor— "Who Should Get In?"

   But instead suppose that the *employers*, rather than immigrants, are the active agents. Suppose their action is to cut wages—outsourcing, or an anti-union campaign, say, or perhaps a legislative maneuver that blocks a rise in the minimum wage and so causes its real value to fall. Now for native workers the worst jobs no longer provide adequate pay. Immigrants may *then* be recruited, directly or through the grapevine, to fill them. They will flood the regions (Los Angeles, Texas) where sweatshops flourish, while remaining scarce in union towns like Detroit. And they will come from low-wage countries, like Mexico.

This sequence has very different implications for policy. For, if only the wage structure had been maintained in the first place—through strong unions, robust minimums, and other measures— then the excess demand for immigrants and the phenomenon of displacement would not occur. It is no coincidence that in 1970 there was no immigrant-native wage differential and yet no migrant wave. The real value of the federal minimum hourly wage, back then, exceeded seven dollars in today's values, and a much higher fraction of the workforce belonged to unions.

James K. Galbraith, letter to the editor,
New York Review of Books, 5/23/2002

Analysis   Galbraith is saying that without substantial research, reversing cause and effect seems just as plausible here, which is sufficient to make us doubt Jenck's conclusion.

Example 26   It's real clear looking at the booms and busts in our economy that they're what swing elections. From 1983 to 1984, real GDP grew by nearly 7 percent, and that helped ensure Ronald Reagan's re-election. But from 1990 to 1991, real GDP fell by 1 percent, which helped Bill Clinton defeat George Bush.

Analysis   The first sentence here is a general causal claim: "The growth (decrease) of GDP is a causal factor in electing (defeating) a presidential candidate." The two particular causal claims (helps = is a causal factor) are no evidence for that, only illustrations, since there's no reason to think they're more than *post hoc* reasoning. Unless "swing" means no more than that the purported cause can be a slight causal factor, we can actually refute the causal claim by noting that the incumbent Al Gore did not soundly defeat George W. Bush in 2000 when real GDP growth was very high.

Example 27   In writing these lines I see the following headlines . . .

     Dow is up 1.03 on lower interest rates

. . . If I translate it well, the journalist claims to provide an explanation for something that amounts to *perfect noise*. A move of 1.03 with the Dow at 11,000 constitutes less than a 0.01% move. Such a move does not warrant an explanation. There is nothing there that an honest person can try to explain; there are no reasons to adduce. But . . . journalists being paid to provide explanations will gladly and readily provide them.

Significance: how did I decide that it was perfect noise? Take a simple analogy. If you engage in a mountain bicycle race with a friend across Siberia and, a month later, beat him by one single second, you clearly cannot boast that you are faster than him. You might have been helped by something, or it can be just plain randomness, nothing else. The second is not in itself significant enough for someone to draw conclusion. I would not write . . . "cyclist A is better than cyclist B because he is fed with spinach whereas cyclist B has a diet rich in tofu. The reason I am making this inference is because he beat him by 1.3 seconds in a 3,000 mile race." Should the difference be one week, then I could start analyzing whether tofu is the reason, of if there are other factors.

Causality; there is another problem; even assuming statistical significance, one has to accept a cause and effect, meaning that the event in the market can be linked to the cause proffered. *Post hoc ergo propter hoc.*

Nassim Taleb, *Fooled by Randomness*

Analysis   Here is someone who has a clear understanding of cause and effect.

4.6 Cause in Populations

In this section we'll learn how to evaluate causal claims when all
we have is a statistical correlation that suggests a causal link.

When we say, "Smoking causes lung cancer," what do we mean? If you smoke a
cigarette, you'll get cancer? If you smoke a lot of cigarettes this week, you'll get cancer?
If you smoke 20 cigarettes a day for 40 years, you'll get cancer? It can't be any of these,
since we know smokers who did all that yet didn't get lung cancer, and the effect must
follow the cause.

Cause in a population is usually explained as meaning that given the cause, there's
a higher probability that the effect will be true than if there were not the cause. In this
example, people who smoke have a much higher probability of getting lung cancer. But
really we are talking about cause and effect just as we did before. Smoking lots of cigarettes
over a long period of time will cause (inevitably) lung cancer. The problem is that we can't
state, we have no idea how to state, nor is it likely that we'll ever be able to state, the normal
conditions for smoking to cause cancer. Among other factors, there is diet, exposure to
pollution and other carcinogens, and one's genetic inheritance. But *if we knew exactly*,
we'd say: "Under the conditions _____ , smoking ___ (number of) cigarettes every day
for ___ years will result in lung cancer."

Since we can't specify the normal conditions, the best we can do is point to the
evidence that convinces us that smoking is a cause of lung cancer and get an argument with a
statistical conclusion: "People who continue to smoke two packs of cigarettes per day for
ten years are ___% more likely (with a margin of error of ___ %) to get lung cancer."

How do we establish cause in a population?

Controlled experiment: *cause-to-effect* This is our best evidence. We choose 10,000
people at random and ask 5,000 of them never to smoke and 5,000 of them to smoke a pack
of cigarettes every day. We have two samples, one composed of those who are administered
the cause, and one of those who are not, the latter called the *control group*. We come back
20 years later to check how many in each group got lung cancer. If a lot more of the
smokers got lung cancer, and the groups were representative of the population as a whole,
and we can see no other *common thread* among those who got lung cancer, we'd be
justified in saying that smoking causes lung cancer.

But such an experiment that is likely to cause harm to people would be unethical, so
researchers use some animals like rats and then argue by analogy.

Uncontrolled experiment: *cause-to-effect* Here we take two randomly chosen,
representative samples of the general population for which we have factored out other
possible causes of lung cancer, such as working in coal mines. One of the groups is

composed of people who say they never smoke. One group is composed of people who say they smoke. We follow the groups and 15 to 20 years later check whether those who smoked got lung cancer more often. Since we think we've accounted for other common threads, smoking is the remaining common thread that may account for why the second group got cancer more often.

This is a cause-to-effect experiment, since we start with the suspected cause and see if the effect follows. But it is uncontrolled: Some people may stop smoking, some may begin, people may have quite variable diets—there may be a lot we'll have to factor out in trying to assess whether it's smoking that caused the extra cases of lung cancer.

Uncontrolled experiment: effect-to-cause   Here we look at as many people as possible who have lung cancer to see if there is some common thread that occurs in (almost all) their lives. We factor out those who worked in coal mines, those who lived in high pollution areas, those who drank a lot, ... If it turns out that a much higher proportion of the remaining people smoked than in the general population, we have good evidence that smoking was the cause (the evaluation of this requires a knowledge of statistics). This is uncontrolled because how they got to the effect was unplanned, not within our control. It is an effect-to-cause experiment because we start with the effect in the population and try to account for how it got there.

Example 1   Barbara smoked two packs of cigarettes each day for thirty years. Barbara now has lung cancer. Barbara's smoking caused her lung cancer.

Analysis   Is it possible for Barbara to have smoked two packs of cigarettes each day for thirty years and not get lung cancer? We can't state the normal conditions. So we invoke the statistical relation between smoking and lung cancer to say it is unlikely for the cause to be true and the effect false.

Does the cause make a difference? Could Barbara have gotten lung cancer even if she had not smoked? Suppose we know that Barbara wasn't a coal miner, didn't work in a textile factory, and didn't live in a city with a very polluted atmosphere—all conditions that are associated with a higher probability of getting lung cancer. It is still possible for Barbara to have gotten lung cancer anyway, since some people who have no other risks do get lung cancer. But it is very unlikely, since very few of those people do.

We have no reason to believe that there is a common cause. It may be that people with a certain biological make-up feel compelled to smoke and that biological make-up also contributes to their getting lung cancer independently of their smoking. But we have no evidence of such a biological factor.

So assuming a few normal conditions, "Barbara's smoking caused her lung cancer" is a claim that is as plausible as the strength of the statistical link between smoking and lung cancer and the strength of the link between not smoking and not getting lung cancer. We must be careful, though, that we do not attribute the cause of the lung cancer to smoking just because we haven't thought of any other cause, especially if the statistical link isn't very strong.

Example 2   Driving over nails causes your tires to go flat.

Analysis   This example is not a true general causal claim: Lots of times we drive over nails and our tires don't go flat. What's true is: Driving over nails *can cause* your tires to go flat. That is, if the conditions are right, driving over a nail will cause your tire to go flat, which is a true cause in population claim.

Example 3 Zoe: I can't understand Melinda. She's pregnant and she's drinking.

> Dick: That's baloney. I asked my mom, and she said she drank when she was pregnant
> with me. And I turned out fine.

> Zoe: But think how much better you would've been if she hadn't.

Analysis Zoe doesn't say but alludes to the cause in population claim that drinking during pregnancy causes birth defects or poor development of the child. That has been demonstrated: Many cause in population studies have been done that show there is a higher incidence of birth defects and developmental problems in children born to mothers who drink than to mothers who do not drink, and those defects and problems do not appear to arise from any other common factor.

But Dick then confuses a cause in population claim with a general causal claim. He's right that his mother's experience would disprove the general causal claim, but it has no force against the cause in population claim.

Zoe's confusion is that she thinks there is a perfect correlation between drinking and mental and physical problems in the child, so that if Dick's mother had not drunk, he would have been better, even if Zoe can't point to the particular way in which Dick would have been better. But the correlation isn't perfect—it's only a statistical link.

Example 4 Lack of education causes poverty. Widespread poverty causes crime. So lack of education causes crime.

Analysis We often hear claims like these, and some politicians base policy on them. But they're too vague. How much education constitutes "lack of education"? How poor do you have to be? How many poor people constitute "widespread poverty"? Researchers make these sentences more precise and analyze them as cause in population claims, since we know they couldn't be true general causal claims: There are people with little education who have become rich; and lots and lots of poor people are law-abiding citizens. Indeed, in the worst years of the Depression in the 1930s, when there was more widespread poverty than at any time since in the U.S., there was less crime than any time in the last 20 years. This suggests it would be hard to find a precise version of the second sentence that is a true cause in population claim.

Example 5 [1] People's expectations about what will happen in the future depend in part on their past experiences. [2] The ways that government has responded to problems in the economy affect how people expect the government to act in the future. So [3] people's expectations about future government actions affect how they respond to current government initiatives. So [4] past responses by the government affect the results of current policies.

Analysis In this passage [1] is a causal claim ("depend" means "are caused in part by"). It might seem like a truism, except we often don't form our expectations about the future from our past experience, hence, the old adage "The triumph of hope over experience." So if it's true, it must be as a cause in population claim, though because of that "in part" it might not amount to much.

Claim [2] is a cause in population claim that seems to follow for those people and situations in which [1] is true. But even if someone always forms his expectations about the future based on past experience, he may not be paying much attention to what the government is doing. So [2] may apply to so few people and situations that [3] and [4] don't follow except in such a weak sense of "affect" that we can say that what you ate three days ago affects what movie you'll choose to see today.

Example 6 "One reason for the persistently higher incidence of poverty among blacks and Hispanics is the lower wage rates earned by workers in these two groups, and this, in turn, is due to discrimination and differences in education levels (which may result from pre-market discrimination). In 1997, for example, 25 percent of the white population had college degrees, but only 13 percent of blacks and 10 percent of Hispanics had graduated from college. In addition to having lower wages, blacks and

Hispanics earn much less nonlabor income than non-Hispanic whites."

    Analysis The first sentence gives a cause in population claim: Lower wage rates earned by blacks and Hispanics is caused by discrimination and differences in education levels. The authors then show that at least in 1997 blacks and Hispanics did have lower education levels than whites. But no further evidence is given for the cause in population claim; in particular no statistical link is cited, so we must accept it solely on the basis of the authors' authority.

Example 7 "Some studies show that teenagers are much more sensitive to cigarette price than adults are. In other words, the elasticity of demand for cigarettes is greater for teenagers than for adults.

    One study found the elasticity of demand for cigarettes to be 0.35 (in the long run). This study did not separate adult smoking and teenage smoking. Another study looked at only teenage smoking and concluded that for every 10 percent rise in price, quantity demanded would decline by 12 percent. In other words, demand for cigarettes by teenagers is elastic."

    Analysis In this passage, a study is used as evidence for the claim that for every 10 percent rise in price, quantity of cigarettes demanded by teenagers will decline by 12 percent. This is neither a general causal claim about teenagers nor a cause in population claim about teenagers, for it does not say that it is certain or even likely that an individual teenager would decrease his or her consumption of cigarettes 12% when there is a 10% increase in price. Rather, it is a general causal claim about supply and demand, each instance of which is a particular causal claim of the sort "On this date the price of cigarettes went up 10%, and on this later date consumption of cigarettes by teenagers went down by 12%."

Example 8 In the last twenty years, as real wages have fallen, the number of people in a family who leave the home each day to earn wages has increased. Moreover, there has recently been a rise in overtime work, that is, people working more than the usual number of hours in their jobs. So reduced real wages seem to have induced people to increase the quantity of labor they supply.

    Analysis This passage presents the claim "Reduced real wages caused people to increase the quantity of labor they supply." That might seem to be a particular causal claim: Real wages went down, which caused an increase in labor in the market. But it's talking about individuals, not society. Yet it is not a general causal claim either, since we all know people who didn't work more during that time. Rather, it is a cause in population claim: Generally, that this wage earner's income was lower in real terms caused him or other members of his family to supply more labor to the market. A correlation is cited to support the claim, but the speaker recognizes that isn't enough by using the word "seem". Other evidence is needed to establish the claim: verifying common causes, verifying the strength of the statistical link, checking that the purported cause made a difference, ...

5   Explanations and Models

Much of the work of economists consists of giving explanations and making predictions. And much of that is accomplished through building models and constructing theories.

To understand models and theories, we first need to be clear about what an explanation is and how to evaluate explanations, which we study in Section 5.1.

Then in Section 5.2 we look at a series of examples of models and theories from science to understand what it means for one theory to be good or better than another.

In the last section of the book we are finally prepared to look at how models and theories function in economics.

5.1 Explanations

In this section we'll learn how to evaluate the kind of explanations
that are meant to answer "Why is this claim true?"

Why does the sun rise in the East? How does electricity work? How come Spot gets a bath every week?

We give explanations as answers to lots of different kinds of questions: Why is this true? How do you do this? What is your motive?

Here we'll look at explanations that are verbal and are meant as answers to the question, "Why is this claim true?" An explanation of that sort is very different from an argument intended to show that the claim is true. For example, an explanation answering "Why does the sun rise in the East?" must assume as obvious that the sun rises in the East; it's not meant to establish that claim, but rather to show that it is true because of some other claims. Here's how we characterize that kind of explanation.

> **Explanations** An **inferential** explanation is a collection of claims that can be understood as "E because of A, B, C, . . .". We call A, B, C, . . . the **explanation** and E the claim that is being explained.
> Sometimes the entire inference itself is called the explanation.

Example 1 —Why is the sky blue?
—Because sunlight is refracted through the air in such a way that other wavelengths are diminished.

    Analysis This is an inferential explanation. The explanation is "Sunlight is refracted through the air in such a way that other wavelengths are diminished"; it is meant to explain "The sky is blue."

Example 2 —Why did the President release oil from the country's emergency stocks this week?
—Because gasoline prices are up 45% this month and he wants to get re-elected in two months.

    Analysis This is an inferential explanation. The explanation consists of two claims, "Gasoline prices are up 45% this month" and "The President wants to get re-elected in two months." These are meant to explain "The President released oil from the country's emergency stocks this week."

What conditions are needed for an explanation to be good?

1. The claim that's meant to be explained is highly plausible.
We can't explain what's not clearly true.

Example 3 Interviewer: Why did the President purposely deceive the public about his tax plan?
    Senator: Hold on. What makes you think he did?

    Analysis The interviewer has posed a loaded question: a request for an explanation of a claim that is not clearly true. The Senator has responded appropriately, asking for an argument to show that "The President purposely deceived the public about his tax plan" is true.

2. *The explanation answers the right question.*
Questions are often ambiguous, and a good explanation to one reading of a question can be a bad explanation to another. If a question is ambiguous, that's a fault of the person asking the question—we can't be expected to guess correctly what's meant. An explanation is bad because it answers the wrong question *if* it's very clear what question is meant.

Example 4 Mother: There were two pieces of cake in the cupboard. Why is there only one now?
    Child: Because it was dark and I couldn't see the other piece.
    Analysis This is a good explanation, but for the wrong question.

3. *The explanation is plausible.*
In an inferential explanation the claims doing the explaining are supposed to make clear why the claim we are explaining is true. They can only do so if they're plausible.

Example 5 The sky is blue because there are blue globules in the atmosphere.
    Analysis This is a bad explanation. We have no reason to believe "There are blue globules in the atmosphere" is true.

Example 6 The stock market went down because a conspiracy among the religious right controls the mutual funds in this country and wants to slow down the economy.
    Analysis This is a bad explanation, since we have no reason to believe that the religious right controls mutual funds in the U.S.

4. *The explanation is valid or strong.*
In an inferential explanation the truth of the claim being explained is supposed to follow from the explanation being true. So the relation between the explanation and the claim that's being explained should be valid or strong, like the relation between the premises and the conclusion of a good argument.

Example 7 The Dow Jones average went below 8000 because of the huge sunspots last week.
    Analysis The inference from "There were huge sunspots last week" to "The Dow Jones average went below 8000" is not obviously valid or strong, so the explanation is bad.

    As with arguments, we allow that an explanation might need repair. An explanation "E because of A" might require further fairly obvious claims to show that it's valid or strong. But a good inferential explanation will have at least one claim in the explanation that is less plausible than what's being explained. Otherwise it wouldn't explain; it would convince. *A good explanation is not a good argument.*

Example 8 Zoe (to Dick): You drank two beers, a bottle of wine with dinner, then three glasses of brandy after dinner. Anyone who drinks that much is going to get a headache.
    Analysis Zoe offers a good explanation of why Dick has a headache:

    Anyone who drinks that much is going to have a headache.
    Therefore (explains why), Dick has a headache.

But judged as an argument this is bad, for it begs the question: It's a lot more obvious to Dick that he has a headache than that anyone who drinks that much is going to have a headache.

5. The explanation is not circular.

We can't explain why a claim is true by just restating the claim in other words.

It's no explanation at all to say, "Unemployment went up 14% because more people were out of work."

We can now sum up the conditions needed for an explanation to be good.

Necessary conditions for an inferential explanation to be good
For "E because of A, B, C, . . ." to be a good inferential explanation:

1. E is highly plausible.

2. A, B, C, . . . answer the right question.

3. Each of A, B, C, . . . is plausible, but at least one of them is not more plausible than E.

4. "A, B, C, . . . therefore E" is valid or strong, possibly with respect to some plausible unstated claims.

5. The explanation is not "E because of D" where D is E itself or a simple rewriting of E.

Causal explanations

Sometimes an explanation is given in terms of cause and effect. If it's good causal reasoning and the explanation answers the right question, then the explanation is good; otherwise it's a bad explanation.

Example 9   Dick woke up because Spot barked.
    Analysis   This is a good explanation that is causal (see pages 74–75).

Example 10   Suzy: Why did the price of gas go up 17% this month?
    Maria: Because OPEC cut the supply by two million barrels per day three weeks ago.
    Analysis   What's missing is a premise that says that supply and cost are always related, which might be used to show that this is a good causal explanation—if there was no common cause.

These next examples illustrate generally how to evaluate an explanation.

Example 11   Customer: Why did you call your coffeehouse *The Dog & Duck*?
    Owner: Because *The Duck & Dog* doesn't sound good.
    Analysis   This is a bad explanation. The inference from "*The Duck & Dog* doesn't sound good" to "I called my coffeehouse *The Dog & Duck*" is weak with no obvious way to repair it.

Example 12   Dick: I don't understand. Why did the President submit a bill to Congress to lower taxes on the wealthiest 1% of taxpayers?
    Tom: Why shouldn't he?
    Analysis   Shifting the burden of proof is just as bad for explanations as for arguments. This is not a bad explanation; it's no explanation at all.

Example 13   Zoe: Why did the Federal Reserve Board lower interest rates?

Dick: Because the rate of investment fell in the last quarter, unemployment was up 14% last month, and they also want to stimulate the economy.

Analysis   This may be a good explanation if it is obvious to Zoe what claims Dick is assuming that make the inference valid or strong. Otherwise, it is bad because it's weak.

Example 14   Suzy: Why did the Federal Reserve Board raise interest rates?

Tom: Because the rate of investment fell in the last quarter, unemployment was up 14% last month, and they also want to stimulate the economy before the election in November.

Analysis   This is a bad explanation—unlike the previous one, we can't even begin to imagine why it would be strong.

Example 15   Suzy: Why did the President disband his Council of Economic Advisors?

Zoe: Because he wanted to.

Analysis   This is a bad explanation. It's obviously true the President wanted to disband his Council of Economic Advisors, and with further premises that will give us "The President disbanded his Council of Economic Advisers." But we want to know *why* the President wanted to do that, which is something unusual and requires further explanation. An explanation is ***inadequate***, and hence bad, if it leads to a further "Why?" Even if the explanation is obviously true, it may not be what we normally expect.

Example 16   —Why was my bid to build the bridge unacceptable?

—Because you didn't have the signatures from the state engineer's office.

Analysis   This is a good explanation if the second person is right. It's an explanation in terms of criteria or rules, which isn't causal.

Example 17   Dr. E: I won't accept your homework late.

Maria: But I had a meeting I had to attend at work.

Dr. E: So? I don't count problems with employment as an adequate excuse for handing in late homework.

Analysis   Maria has explained why she did not hand in the homework on time. She thinks she's also given an excuse, but Dr. E disagrees. What your employer will count as an excuse for being late may be unclear until you try a couple. What counts to a police officer as an excuse for speeding is very limited. *A good explanation need not be a good excuse.*

The relation of explanations to arguments

Dick, Zoe, and their dog Spot are out for a walk in the countryside. Spot runs off and returns after five minutes. Dick notices that Spot has blood around his muzzle. And both Zoe and Dick really notice that Spot stinks like a skunk. Dick turns to Zoe and says, "Spot must have killed a skunk. Look at the blood on his muzzle. And he smells like a skunk."

Dick has made a *good argument*:

Spot has blood on his muzzle. Spot smells like a skunk.
Therefore, Spot killed a skunk.

Dick has left out some premises that he knows are as obvious to Zoe as to him:

Spot isn't bleeding.
Skunks aren't able to fight back very well.

Normally when Spot draws a lot of blood from an animal that is smaller than him, he kills it.

Only skunks give off a characteristic odor that drenches whoever or whatever is near if they are attacked.

Dogs kill animals by biting them and typically drawing blood.

Zoe replies, "Oh, that explains why he's got blood on his muzzle and smells so bad." That is, she takes the same claims and views them as an explanation, a *good explanation*, relative to the same unstated premises:

Spot killed a skunk.

Therefore (explains why) Spot has blood on his muzzle and smells like a skunk.

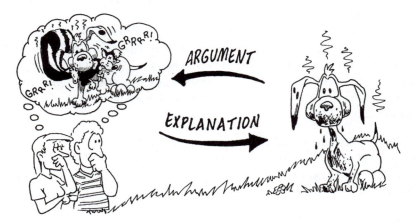

Suppose we have an explanation "Y *explains* X", perhaps relative to some other claims P, Q, R, ... We can ask what evidence we have for Y. Sometimes we can supply all the evidence we need to show that Y is plausible by simply reversing the inference, using the ***associated argument***: "X *therefore* Y (with additional premises P, Q, R, . . .)". In this example, for Zoe's explanation to be good, "Spot killed a skunk" must be plausible. And it is, because of the associated argument that Dick gave. More often, however, we have to supplement an explanation with further plausible claims.

Example 18 Spot chases cats because he sees cats as something good to eat and because cats are smaller than him.

Analysis "Cats are smaller than Spot" is plausible, but "Spot sees cats as something good to eat" is not obviously true. The associated argument for it is the following:

Spot chases cats and cats are smaller than Spot.

Therefore, Spot sees cats as something good to eat.

This is weak. Without more evidence for "Spot sees cats as something good to eat" we shouldn't accept the explanation.

Example 19 "The classical statement of this view of stock market behavior was provided in 1936 by English economist John Maynard Keynes, a professional speculator himself:

'Professional investment may be likened to those newspaper competitions in which the competitors have to pick out the six prettiest faces from a hundred photographs, the prize being awarded to the competitor whose choice most nearly corresponds to the average preferences of the competitors as a whole; so that each competitor has to pick out not those faces which he himself finds prettiest, but those which he thinks likeliest to catch the fancy of the other competitors, all of whom are looking at the problem from the same point of view. It is not the case of choosing those which, to the best of one's judgment, are really the prettiest, nor even those which average opinion genuinely thinks the prettiest. We have reached the third degree where we devote our intelligences to anticipating what average opinion expects the average opinion to be. And there are some, I believe, who practice the fourth, fifth and higher degrees.'

This may help to explain the impressive rise of the stock market from a Dow Jones index of 800 in 1982 to 2700 in 1987, a 700 point fall in two consecutive trading days in October 1987, then several sharp fluctuations followed by a remarkably sustained upward trend since then."

Analysis The authors are careful to say that the passage from Keynes *may help* to explain the fluctuations in the stock market. More evidence, beyond just the cited numbers of the Dow Jones index, is needed to establish that the comparison does apply to stock market traders. Also, further claims are needed to show that the inference is valid or strong.

Explanations and predictions

Example 20 Flo: Spot barks. And Wanda's dog Ralph barks. And Dr. E's dogs Anubis and Juney bark. So all dogs bark.

Barb: Yeah. Let's go over to Maple Street and see if all the dogs there bark, too.

Analysis Flo, who's five, is generalizing. Her friend Barb wants to test the generalization.

Suppose that A, B, C, D are given as inductive evidence for a generalization G. (Some other plausible unstated premises may also be needed, but we'll keep those in the background.) Then we have that G explains A, B, C, D.

But if G is true, we can see that some other claims must be true—instances of the generalization G, say L, M, N. If those are true, then G would explain them, too. (In the last example, Birta barks, Buddy barks, Fido barks, ...) That is, G *explains* A, B, C, D and *predicts* L, M, N, where the difference between the explanation and the prediction is that in the explanation we know that the claim being explained is true, whereas we don't know if the prediction is true.

Suppose we find that L, M, N are indeed true. Then the argument "A, B, C, D + L, M, N, therefore G" is a better argument for G than we had before. At the very least it has more instances of the generalization as premises.

How can more instances of a generalization prove the generalization better? They can if (1) they are from different kinds of situations, that is, A, B, C, D + L, M, N cover a more representative sample of possible instances of G than do just A, B, C, D. This is typically what happens. We deduce claims from G for situations that we had not previously considered.

And (2), because we had not previously considered the kind of instances L, M, N of the generalization G, we have some confidence that we haven't gotten G by manipulating the data, selecting situations that would establish just this hypothesis.

One of the best ways to test a hypothesis-generalization is to try to falsify it. Trying to falsify the generalization means that we are consciously trying to come up with instances of the generalization to test that are as different as we can imagine from A, B, C, D. Trying to falsify is a good way to ensure (1) and (2). We say an experiment *confirms*—to some extent—the (doubtful claims in the) explanation if it shows that a prediction is true.

Comparing explanations

Given two explanations of the same claim, which is better? If one is right and the other wrong, the right one is better. If both are acceptable, we prefer the one that answers the right question and that doesn't leave us asking a further "Why?"

We also prefer a *simpler* explanation: its premises are more plausible, it is more clearly strong or valid (unstated premises are obvious and more plausible), and it has fewer steps. All else being equal, we also prefer the stronger of two explanations.

There are other ways to compare explanations, too, but at present these are all the criteria that people agree on.

Example 21   Zoe: How was your walk?
Dick: Spot ran away again just a little ways from the yard.
Zoe: We better get him. Why does he run away right before you get home?
Dick: It's just his age. He'll outgrow it. All dogs do.
Analysis   This sounded like a good explanation until Dick and Zoe found that Spot chased a cat up a telephone pole in the field behind their house.

The explanation in this example is not bad. Perhaps in a year or two when Spot is better trained, he won't run away even to chase a cat. But there is a better explanation—one that is stronger: Spot ran away because he likes to chase cats.

Some scientists think that if an explanation is better than any other one around and the explanation could explain a lot, then the explanation must be true.

Example 22   It can hardly be supposed that a false theory would explain, in so satisfactory a manner as does the theory of natural selection, the several large classes of facts above specified [the geographical distribution of species, the existence of vestigial organs in animals, etc.]. It has recently been objected that this is an unsafe method of arguing; but it is a method used in judging of the common events of life, and has often been used by the greatest natural philosophers."

                                        Charles Darwin, *On the Origin of Species*

Analysis   If Darwin was right, why did scientists spend the next hundred years trying to confirm or disprove the hypothesis of natural selection? Only now do we believe that a somewhat revised version of Darwin's hypotheses are true.

Saying that a claim is true because it would explain a lot is arguing backwards: From the premises (explanation) we can argue to true claims, so the premises are true. That kind of reasoning doesn't get any better by adding, "This is the best explanation", because we don't have accepted criteria for what counts as the best explanation.

> **Fallacy of inference to the best explanation**   It is bad reasoning to argue that because some claims constitute the best explanation they are therefore true.

Scientists have high hopes for their hypotheses and are motivated to investigate them if they appear to provide a better explanation than current theories. But the scientific community quickly corrects anyone who thinks that just making an hypothesis establishes it as true.

This the best explanation we have = This is a good hypothesis to investigate

Example 23 Maria: Why do I have such pain in my back? It doesn't feel like a muscle cramp or a pinched nerve.

Doctor: A kidney stone would explain the pain. Kidney stones give that kind of pain, and it's in the right place for that.

Analysis The doctor's explanation is "Your back hurts because you have a kidney stone." This would have been a good explanation if the doctor and Maria had good reason to believe it. But at that point the only reason they had was the associated argument, which wasn't strong. Still, it was the best explanation at the time.

So the doctor made predictions from the explanation: "A kidney stone would show up on an X-ray," "You would have an elevated white-blood cell count," and "You would have blood in your urine." He tested each of these and found them false. If the explanation were true, each would very likely be true. Therefore, (reducing to the absurd) the explanation is very likely false.

Nothing else was found, so by process of elimination the doctor concluded that Maria had a severe sprain or strain, for which exercise and education were the only remedy. The doctor was right to investigate whether the best explanation he had at the time was really true before he did surgery.

Here are some examples to work through that illustrate some of these ideas.

Example 24 —Why will the stock market go up next quarter?

—Because all the economic indicators are up and the Fed has lowered interest rates.

Analysis This sounds like an explanation, but it isn't: "The stock market will go up next quarter" is not obviously true. It's a prediction. If it comes true, then that would be further evidence for the general claim "[Usually?] when all the economic indicators are up and the Fed reduces interest rates, the stock market rises."

Example 25 —Why is the missile going off in that direction?

—Because it wants to hit that plane.

Analysis It's a bad *anthropomorphism* to ascribe goals to a missile: People, not missiles, have goals. We can and should replace this explanation: The missile has been designed to go in the direction of the nearest source of heat comparable to the heat generated by a jet engine. The plane over in that direction has a jet engine producing that kind of heat. So (that explains why) the missile went in that direction.

Example 26 The agricultural labourer, the industrial worker and so on *consume less than they produce*—because they are *compelled* to sell most of the produce of their labour and to be satisfied with but a small portion of it.

Kropotkin, The Conquest of Bread

Analysis This explanation needs to be supplemented: Kropotkin has to show why it's true that workers are compelled to sell most of the produce of their labor.

Example 27 Zoe: Why did Mr. Johns, the owner of that fast-food restaurant where you work, lower prices on all the meals?

Suzy: It's because he's got a good heart and wants poor people to be able to enjoy his food.

Zoe: I don't think so. He was the one who opposed soup kitchens in town.

Zoe: (*Later*) I read in the newspaper that Mr. Johns said he lowered his prices because he had to beat the prices of those two other fast-food restaurants up the block.

Suzy: He's just covering up. He's afraid of being thought a nice guy. He can't face his unconscious wish to be loved.

Analysis   Is Suzy's explanation good? All the evidence Zoe has points to the explanation being false. Of course what Suzy says could be true. But there's no way to test whether that's Mr. Johns' motive, since he's either hiding it or it's unconscious.

Untestable claims are the worst candidates for a good explanation. Claims about hidden or unconscious motivation particularly are a dime a dozen and can explain anything; they just can't explain anything well.

Example 28   "Economic efficiency can be a powerful tool to help us understand the economic changes that shook the world in the late 1980s and early 1990s. It can also help us understand the changes that are continuing to take place in China in the year 2000 and beyond, and may—in the future—take place in such holdouts as Cuba, Belarus, and North Korea as well. Simply put, the system that these nations had in place for decades—centrally planned socialism—was economically inefficient. True, the Soviet-inspired system of resource allocation by command and resource ownership by the state had its advantages. But the system was plagued by so much inefficiency that—far from achieving its goals of beating living standards in market economies—it collapsed."

Analysis   This passage gives a causal explanation of why there were major economic changes in the late 1980s and early 1990s. By this we suppose the authors mean that many countries during that period abandoned the communist organization of their economies and also adopted more transparent democracies. The authors follow this passage with a description of the Soviet economy and show that it was indeed inefficient, but that's only an illustration, not a proof that the explanation is true. They also point out that starting in the 1980s the standard of living in the Soviet Union began to fall relative to the standard in the West, and due to improved communications "Soviet citizens became more and more disaffected and cynical about their own system."

But does this explain why the Soviet Union abandoned communism? The people there had been fed up with the inefficiency of the system and the hypocrisy of their leaders for more than a generation. In any case, the changes did not come from the ordinary people. The authors haven't established that the cause they suggest really made a difference. What was unusual during that period was that the leadership of the Soviet Union under Gorbachev allowed open discussion of the problems of the economy and, more importantly, of the government. At best, the inefficiency of the economy was part of the cause, part of the explanation, of why the Soviet Union abandoned communism.

Example 29   There are, in general, eight main motives or objects of a subjective character which lead individuals to refrain from spending out of their incomes: . . .

> (iv) To enjoy a gradually increasing expenditure, since it gratifies a common instinct to look forward to a gradually improving standard of life rather than the contrary, even though the capacity for enjoyment may be diminishing.   Keynes, *The General Theory of Employment*

Analysis   Many of the assumptions and principles of economic models that you'll study are propounded on the basis of no more than "armchair psychology": they seem obvious, and no experiments/observations are cited. When you read something like (iv), ask yourself why you should believe it. Only recently have economists trained in psychology begun to make contributions to framing economic models.

5.2 Models and Theories

What is a model? How do we determine if a model is good? How can we modify a model in the light of new evidence? In this section we'll look at these questions through a series of examples from ordinary life and science, before turning to models in economics in the next section.

Example 1   A map of Minersville, Utah—a model is used for reasoning by analogy

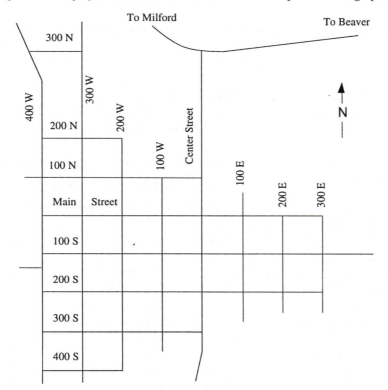

We can see from this map that the streets are evenly spaced, for example, there is the same distance between 100 N and 200 N as between 100 E and 200 E. To the east, the last street is 300 E. There's no paved road going north beyond Main Street on 200 E.

That is, from this map we can deduce claims about Minersville, even if we've never been there. But there's much we can't deduce: Are there hills in Minersville? Are there lots of trees? How wide are the streets? How far apart are the streets? Where are houses located?

Reasoning about Minersville from this map is reasoning by analogy. The map is similar to Minersville in the relative position of streets and their orientation to north. The differences between the map and Minersville aren't important when we infer that the north end of 200 W is at 200 N. The map is accurate for what it pays attention to, but is not informative about what it ignores.

In contrast, a scale model of a city or a landscape *abstracts less* from the actual terrain: height and often placements of rivers and trees are shown. A model *models more* if there are more similarities between the model and what it is modeling. The map of Minersville *abstracts more* from the actual terrain than a scale model of the city would: it ignores more.

This example highlights that *models are used for analogies*: *We can draw conclusions when appropriate similarities are noted and the differences don't matter.* The general principle, in this example, is not stated explicitly. The discussion above suggests how we might formulate one, but it hardly seems worth the effort. We can "see" when someone has used a map well or badly.

Example 2   The kinetic theory of gases—getting true predictions doesn't mean the model is "true"

This theory is based on the following postulates, or assumptions.

1. Gases are composed of a large number of particles that behave like hard, spherical objects in a state of constant, random motion.
2. The particles move in a straight line until they collide with another particle or the walls of the container.
3. The particles are much smaller than the distance between the particles. Most of the volume of a gas is therefore empty space.
4. There is no force of attraction between gas particles or between the particles and the walls of the container.
5. Collisions between gas particles or collisions with the walls of the container are perfectly elastic. Energy can be transferred from one particle to another during a collision, but the total kinetic energy of the particles after the collision is the same as it was before the collision.
6. The average kinetic energy of a collection of gas particles depends on the temperature of the gas and nothing else.

J. Spencer, G. Bodner, and L. Rickard, *Chemistry*

Here is a picture of what is supposed to be going on in a gas in a closed container.
The molecules of gas are represented as dots, as if they were hard spherical balls. The length of the line emanating from a particle models the particle's speed; the arrow models the direction the particle is moving. The kinetic energy of a particle is defined in terms of its mass and velocity: kinetic energy = .5 mass x velocity^2.

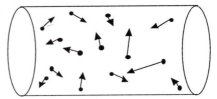

The model defines what is meant for a collision to be elastic. In contrast, here is a picture of what happens in an inelastic collision between a rubber ball and the floor.
Each time the ball hits the ground, some of its kinetic energy is lost either through being transferred to the floor or in compressing the ball.

The kinetic theory of gases abstracts very much from what a gas in a container actually is: Molecules of gas are not generally spherical and are certainly not solid; the collisions between molecules and the walls of a container or each other are not perfectly elastic; there is some gravitational attraction between the particles and each other and also with the container.
That is, there are a lot of differences.

But there are enough similarities for the model to be useful. The model suggests that the pressure of a gas results from the collisions between the gas particles and the walls of the container. So if the container is made smaller for the same amount of gas, the pressure should increase; and vice versa, if the container is made larger, the pressure should be less. So the pressure should be proportional to the inverse of the volume of the gas. That is, the model suggests a claim about the relationship of pressure to volume in a gas. Experiments can be performed, varying the pressure or volume, and they are close to being in accord with that claim.

Other laws are also suggested by the model: Pressure is proportional to the temperature of the gas, where the temperature is taken to be the average kinetic energy of the gas. The volume of the gas should be proportional to the temperature. The amount of gas should be proportional to the pressure. All of these are confirmed by experiment.

Those experiments confirming predictions from the model do not mean that the model is more accurate than we thought. Collisions still aren't really elastic; molecules aren't really hard spherical balls. The kinetic theory of gases is a model of a process, useful where the differences don't matter.

Example 3   The acceleration of falling objects—an entirely mathematical model
Galileo argued that falling objects accelerate as they fall: They begin falling slowly and fall faster and faster the farther they fall. He didn't need any mathematics to demonstrate that. He just noted that a heavy stone dropped from 6 meters will drive a stake into the ground much farther than if it were dropped from 6 centimeters.

Galileo also said the reason that a feather falls more slowly than an iron ball when dropped is because of the resistance of air. He argued that at a given location on the earth and in the absence of air resistance, all objects should fall with the same acceleration. He claimed further that the distance traveled by a falling object is proportional to the square of the time it travels. Today, from many measurements, the equation is given by:

(*) $d = 9.80 \text{ meters}/_{\text{sec}^2} \cdot t^2$ where t is measured in seconds

For example, if you drop a ball from the Empire State Building, after 4 seconds it should travel:

$d = 9.80 \text{ meters}/_{\text{sec}^2} \cdot (4 \text{ sec})^2 = 9.80 \text{ meters} \cdot 16 = 156.8 \text{ meters}$

The equation (*) is an analogy. It says that if we compare a falling object to an imaginary point mass falling to the earth with no air resistance, then the calculation from the equation, which is really a deduction, will hold for the object, too. The differences don't matter. Or rather, they don't matter very much, since air resistance does slow down an object: If you drop a hat from an airplane, it will reach a maximum velocity when the force of the air resistance equals the force of acceleration. And it matters, too, where on earth you are: An object dropped from a 100-foot building in San Francisco at near sea level will accelerate more than an object dropped from a 100-foot building in Denver at 5000 feet above sea level. We can draw conclusions from the analogy when the differences don't matter.

With this model there is no visual representation of that part of experience that is being described—no point-to-point conceptual comparison. The model is couched in the language of mathematics; equations can be models, too.

Example 4   Newton's laws of motion and Einstein's theory of relativity—
How can a false theory be applied?
Newton's laws of motion are taught in every elementary physics course and are used daily by physicists. Yet modern physics has replaced Newton's theories with Einstein's and quantum mechanics. Newton's laws, physicists tell us, are false.

But can't we say that Newton's laws are correct relative to the quality of measurements involved, even though Newton's laws can't be derived from quantum mechanics? Or perhaps they can if a premise is added that we ignore certain small effects. Yet how is that part of a theory?

A theory is a schematic representation of some part of the world, just as a model is.
We draw conclusions from the representation (we calculate or deduce). The conclusion is said
to apply to the world. The reasoning is legitimate so long as the differences between the
representation and what is being represented don't matter. Newton's laws of motion are "just like" how moderately large objects interact at moderately low speeds; we can use those laws to make calculations so long as the differences don't matter. Some of the assumptions of that theory are used as conditions to tell us when the theory is meant to be applied.

Example 5 Ether as the medium of propagation of light waves—a prediction can show an
assumption of a theory is false

In the 19th century light was understood as waves. In analogy with waves in water or sound waves in the air, a medium was postulated for the propagation of light waves: the ether. Using that assumption, many predictions could be made about the path of light in terms of its wave behavior. Attempts were made to isolate or verify the existence of an ether. But the predictions that were made turned out to be false. When a better theory was postulated by Einstein, one which assumed no ether and gave as good or better predictions in all cases where the ether assumption did, the theory of ether was abandoned.

Example 6 Euclidean plane geometry—a model that can't be true

Euclidean plane geometry speaks of points and lines: a point is location without dimension, a line is extension without breadth. No such objects exist in our experience. But Euclidean geometry is remarkably useful in measuring and calculating distances and positions in our daily lives.

Points are abstractions of very small dots made by a pencil or other implement. Lines are abstractions of physical lines, either drawn or sighted. So long as the differences don't matter, that is, so long as the size of the points and the lines are very small relative to what is being measured or plotted, we can deduce conclusions that are true.

No one asks (anymore) whether the axioms of Euclidean geometry are true. Rather, when the differences don't matter, we can calculate and predict using Euclidean geometry. When the differences do matter, as in calculating paths of airplanes circling the globe, Euclidean plane geometry does not apply, and another model, geometry for spherical surfaces, is invoked.

Euclidean geometry is a deductive theory: A conclusion drawn from the axioms is accepted only if the inference is valid. It is a purely mathematical theory, which taken as mathematics would appear to have no application since the objects of which it speaks do not exist. But taken as a model, it has applications in the usual sense, arguing by analogy where the differences don't matter.

Example 7 Classical propositional logic—a prescriptive model

Suppose we ignore everything about claims except whether they are true or false and how they are built up as compounds using the words "and", "or", and "not". We use the symbols &, ∨, and ~ to stand for these abstracted versions of "and", "or", and "not", according to the following tables for the classical understanding of how the truth-value of a compound relates to the truth-value of its parts. Here A, B stand for claims, and T stands for "true", while F stands for "false".

A	B	A & B		A	B	A ∨ B		A	~A
T	T	T		T	T	T		T	F
T	F	F		T	F	T		F	T
F	T	F		F	T	T			
F	F	F		F	F	F			

Using these tables repeatedly, we can calculate the truth-value of any compound claim built using "and", "or", and "not" if we know the truth-values of its parts. For example, "Either Ralph is a dog or Howie is not a cat, and also George is a duck, but Birta is not a dog" would correspond to:

(A ∨ ~B) & (C & ~D)

Using these determinations, we can model whether one claim follows validly as conclusion from other claims. It must be impossible for all the premises to be true and the conclusion false at the same time, which is the case based solely on the form of the propositions (relative to "and", "or", "not") if there is no assignment of truth-values to the premises that makes all of them true and the conclusion false.

This model or theory of reasoning is quite different from the other models we've seen. As a model of reasoning, its role is ***prescriptive***. It says that this is the correct way to reason. It is not the worse for finding that people do not reason as it describes.

Or rather, it says that this is the correct way to reason so long as the differences don't matter. But if the differences do matter, for example, if we wish to suspend judgment on some claims and see where that leads us, then this model won't be useful for drawing conclusions about how we should reason.

Models and analogies

We have seen models of static situations (the map) and of processes (acceleration of falling objects). We have seen examples of models that are entirely visual and of models formulated entirely in terms of mathematical equations. We have seen models in which the assumptions of the model are entirely implicit (the map), and we have seen models in which the assumptions are quite explicit (Newton's laws of motion). Above all, we have seen how to reason with models.

> **Reasoning with models**   Models are used to reason by analogy. We can draw conclusions based on the similarities, so long as the differences don't matter.

We do not ask whether the assumptions of the model are true, but whether we can use the model in the given situation: Do the similarities that are being invoked hold, and do the differences not matter? Even in the case of Newton's laws of motion, where it would seem that what is at stake is whether the assumptions are true, we continue to use the model when we know that the assumptions are false in those cases where, as in any analogy, the differences don't matter. In only one example (the ether) did it seem that what was at issue was whether a particular assumption of the theory was actually true of the world.

The assumptions of theories in science are false when we consider them as representing *all* aspects of some particular part of our experience. The key claim in every analogy is false in the same way. When we say that one side of an analogy is "just like" the other, that's false. What is true is that they are "like" one another in some key respects which allow us to deduce claims for the one from deducing claims for the other.

The term *model* is typically applied to what can be visualized or made concrete, while the term *theory* seems to be used for examples that are fairly formal with explicitly stated assumptions. But in many cases it is as appropriate to call an example a theory as to call it a model, and there seems to be no definite distinction between those terms.

Confirming a theory

From theories we can make predictions, and we say that when a prediction turns out to be true it **confirms** (to some degree) the theory. But this is not the same as confirming an explanation, for it rarely makes sense to say the claims that make up a theory—the assumptions of the theory—are true or false.

We cannot say that verifications of the relation of pressure, temperature, and volume in a gas confirm that molecules are hard little balls and that all collisions are completely elastic. We cannot say that a T-square fitting exactly into a wooden triangle that is 5cm x 4cm x 3cm confirms the theorem of Pythagoras. Nor can we say that finding a tree at the corner of 100 W and 100 S in Minersville disconfirms the model given by the map. The map wasn't meant to give any information about trees, so it doesn't matter that it shows no tree there.

Except in rare instances where we think (usually temporarily) that we have hit upon a truth of the universe to use as an assumption in a theory, such as $e = mc^2$, we do not think that the assumptions of a theory are true or false. We can only say of a theory such as Euclidean plane geometry or the kinetic theory of gases whether it is ***applicable*** in a particular situation we are investigating.

To say that a theory is applicable is to say that though there are differences between the world and what the assumptions of the theory state, those differences don't matter for the conclusions we wish to draw. Often we can decide if a theory is applicable only by attempting to apply it. We use the theory to draw conclusions in particular instances, claiming that the differences don't matter. If the conclusions—the predictions—turn out to be true (enough), then we have some confidence that we are right. If a prediction turns out false, then the model is not applicable there. We do not say that Euclidean plane geometry is false because it cannot be used to calculate the path of an airplane on the globe; we say that Euclidean plane geometry is inapplicable for calculating on globes.

When we make predictions and they are true, we confirm a range of application of a model. When we make predictions and they are false, we disconfirm a range of application, that is, we find limits for the range of application of a model. More information about where the model can be applied and where it cannot be applied may lead, often with great effort, to our describing more precisely the range of application of a model. In that case, the claims describing the range of application can be added to the theory. We often use mathematics as a language for making this art of analogy precise. For example, for Newton's laws of motion we can give limits on the size and speed of objects for which the theory is applicable. But in many cases it is difficult to state precisely the range of application. Reasoning using models is reasoning by analogy, after all, and that is likely to require judgment. In other cases, such as the map of Minersville, it hardly seems worthwhile to state explicitly the range of application.

Sometimes it's said that a theory is valid, or is true, or that a theory holds, or that a theory works for, ... These are just different ways to assert that a particular situation or class of situations to which we wish to apply a theory is within the range of that theory.

Good theories and modifying theories in the light of new evidence
We've seen that the criteria for whether a theory is good or better than another cannot in general include whether the assumptions of the theory are true or "realistic".

Some people say the sole criterion for judging whether a theory is good is whether it yields sufficiently accurate predictions. Certainly it is important to get good predictions. But if the assumptions of the theory are neither true nor true for the situation being analyzed, on what should we base our acceptance of further predictions? A good track record in the past? But who has been keeping score? Perhaps it is just judicious uses of the theory, always supplemented with other assumptions—often unstated—that result in predictions that are sufficiently accurate. What allows us to distinguish between astrology and a theory that makes good predictions yet whose assumptions are clearly false? After all, for many centuries astrology was the best theory around for divining people's fate. Its predictions often came true, since they were sufficiently vague to allow that. And few people were keeping track of the predictions that turned out false.

But besides getting true predictions, what other criteria can we use to evaluate a theory? Consider what we do when we discover that a prediction made from a theory is false.

When Newton's laws of motion result in inaccurate predictions for very small objects, we note that the theory had been assumed true for all sizes of objects and then restrict the range of application.

On the other hand, when the theory of the ether resulted in false predictions, no modification was made to the theory, for none could be made. That theory did not abstract from experience, ignoring some aspects of situations under consideration, but postulated something in addition to our experience, something we were able to show did not exist. The theory was completely abandoned.

Generally, if a theory has been made by abstraction, that is, many aspects of our experience are ignored and only some few are considered significant, then tracing back along that *path of abstraction* we can try to distinguish what difference there is between our model and our experience that matters. What have we ignored that cannot in this situation be ignored? If we cannot state generally what the difference is that matters, then at best the false prediction sets some limit on the range of applicability of the model or theory. We cannot use the theory here—where "here" means this situation or ones that we can see are very similar.

But our goal will be to state precisely the difference that matters and try to factor it into our theory. That is, we try to devise a complication of our theory in which that aspect of our experience is taken into account. As with Einstein's improvement of Newton's laws, we get a better theory that is more widely applicable and which explains why the old theory worked as well as it did and why it failed in the ways it failed. We improve the map: By adding further assumptions, we can pay attention to more in our experience, and that accounts for the differences between the theories.

True predictions are never enough to justify a theory. Indeed, the problem is that we do not "justify" a theory, nor show that it is "valid". What we do in the process of testing predictions is show how and where the theory can be applied. And for us to have confidence in that, either we must show that the claims in the theory are true or show in what situations the differences between what is represented and the abstraction of it in the theory do not matter. True (enough) predictions help in that. But equally crucial is our ability to trace the path of abstraction so that we can see what has been ignored in our reasoning and why true predictions serve to justify our ignoring those aspects of experience. Without that clear path of abstraction, all we can do is try to prove that the claims in the theory are actually true. Without that clear path or reason to believe the claims are true, we have no more reason to trust the predictions of a theory than we have to trust the predictions of astrology.

Sometimes we may be confronted with two theories that both yield good predictions for a class of situations and which both have a clear path of abstraction. In that case, we say that *one theory is **better*** than another (i) the simpler the assumptions, (ii) the clearer the derivations of the claims it is meant to explain, (iii) the wider the range of application, and (iv) the better the explanations it yields of the archetypal claims it is meant to explain.

5.3 Models in Economics

Models and theories in economics are used not only to arrive at truths about the world, but also to try to control the future through economic policy. In this section we'll look at the kinds of assumptions that are built into economic models in order to help you understand the particular models you'll see in your economics courses.

In economics, someone is said to be acting "rationally" if he or she is acting in accord with his or her own self-interest.

> "The assumption that individuals act to advance their goals—known as the rule of rational choice—merely implies that whatever individuals do, they do with a purpose. In economics we assume that each individual seeks to maximize his or her own self-interest."

But what does "self-interest" mean? The idea entered into economics with Adam Smith in his *Wealth of Nations*:

> It is not from the benevolence of the butcher, the brewer, or the baker that we expect our dinner, but from their regard to their own interest.

Self-interest means what we ordinarily think it does: It is contrasted with benevolence.

Some economists find this notion too restrictive. They recognize that people sometimes want to give to charity or help their neighbors, and they allow "self-interest" to include those kinds of goals also. But that's too broad, for then every action is self-interested. For example,

Zoe: I can't believe you gave our take-out dinner to that beggar.
Dick: It seemed like the right thing to do.
Zoe: Oh, c'mon. You just did it to make yourself feel better.

So economists limit the idea. They typically quantify self-interest using the best measuring tool they have: money and the willingness to pay.

> The advantage which economics has over other branches of social science appears then to arise from the fact that its special field of work gives rather larger opportunities for exact methods than any other branch. It concerns itself chiefly with those desires, aspirations and other affections of human nature, the outward manifestation of which appear as incentives to action in such a form that the force or quantity of the incentives can be estimated and measured with some approach to accuracy; and which therefore are in some degree amenable to treatment by scientific machinery. An opening is made for the methods and the tests of science as soon as the person's motives—*not* the motives themselves—can be approximately measured by the sum of money, which he will just give up in order to secure a desired satisfaction; or again by the sum which is just required to induce him to undergo a certain fatigue.
>
> Alfred Marshall, *Principles of Economics*

To define discrimination I use the economic concept of willingness to pay, which is crucial in all parts of economics.   Gary Becker, interview with the Federal Reserve Bank

Acting in accord with self-interest is typically taken to mean acting to maximize profit (or expected profit).

Example 1 "The least-cost solution would have the seller [of the used car] reveal his superior information to a potential buyer. The problem is that it is not individually rational for the seller to provide a truthful and complete disclosure, and this is known by a potential buyer."

Analysis Ethically it is wrong to lie. But if all we are noting is whether the person is acting in accord with self-interest, it may be rational to lie. This might not be what you understand by "rational", but it's how economists use the word.

Economists also use the term "rational" to describe people whose preferences satisfy certain conditions.

"One common denominator—and a critical assumption behind consumer theory— is that people *have* preferences. More specifically, we assume that you can look at two alternatives and state that you prefer one to the other or that you are entirely indifferent between the two—you value them equally.

Another common denominator is that preferences are *logically consistent*, or *transitive*. If, for example, you prefer a sports car to a jeep, and a jeep to a motorcycle, then we assume that you will also prefer a sports car to a motorcycle. When a consumer's preferences are logically consistent in this manner, we say that she has *rational preferences*.

Notice that rationality is a matter of how you make your choices, and *not what choices you make*. . . . What matters is that you make choices consistently, and most of us usually do. Imagine for a moment what it might be like if you didn't. How would you figure out what to order in a restaurant if you prefer the chef's salad to the Reuben sandwich and the Reuben sandwich to the hamburger, but prefer the hamburger to the chef's salad! Clearly, choosing consistently is an important part of just being able to choose."

Whether you think these conditions for having preferences are logical or not, it's important to remember that this is how economists use the term "rational (logical) preferences" in the books and articles you'll read.

An additional notion of rationality that economists use is similar to a criterion that is sometimes proposed for reasoning: A rational person is one who takes into account all relevant information available to him or her.

"What is a sensible way to treat expectations in economics? The rational-expectation theorists answer this question with the *rational-expectations hypothesis*. According to rational expectations, forecasts are unbiased and are based on all available information."

Further, economists require that a rational person be one who reasons correctly. This is a stronger condition than is built into our Principle of Rational Discussion.

In summary, then, economists typically use the word "rational" to mean that all four of these conditions apply.

> **People are rational** means *in economics* that:
>
> 1. They are motivated solely by self-interest.
> 2. They have fixed, transitive preferences.
> 3. They use all the information available to them.
> 4. They reason correctly.

In ordinary language the term "rational" always connotes approval. But in economics no value judgment is meant. It's used solely to describe people and situations to which particular theories or models apply. From the assumption of rationality, economists can draw many conclusions.

Of course not everyone is interested all the time in maximizing his or her own satisfaction. Nor do people always reason correctly. But then molecules aren't hard spherical balls, either. *The question in applying a model based on the assumption of rationality is whether the differences matter, whether a good abstraction has been made.*

Example 2 INGAA [Interstate Natural Gas Association of America] is actively pursuing a pipeline safety program that promotes greater public knowledge of the industry's excellent safety record and minimizes unnecessary regulations and legislation. INGAA will continue to pursue natural gas pipeline safety integrity rules that are *rational*, cost-effective and flexible; provide input on a community outreach rule that assures the public that natural gas pipelines are safe, and to incorporate efforts pipelines already in use [sic]; use the Internet to inform the public on pipeline safety; and work to assure that any Congressional actions to legislate pipeline safety make sense and are cost-effective.

www.ingaa.org/safety/index.php?page=main, 7/24/02 [italics added]

Analysis This passage suggests that the INGAA is acting in the public's interest. But if "rational" here is meant in the economists' sense of acting in accord with self-interest, then they have said that they'll only make corrections if they can make money doing so.

Example 3 Bob decides to sell his land now in order to make $20,000, even though he knows he can make $41,000 from it six months later. Is he acting rationally?

Analysis When we ask whether someone is rational in the sense of maximizing profit, we implicitly assume some time frame. Clear-cutting trees on a large piece of forest and not replanting maximizes profits in the short term, though it might not in the long term.

Example 4 "Police activity and other crime prevention measures are examples of *public goods*. These goods and services . . . have characteristics that make private market production of them inefficient. First of all, public goods are *indivisible*, which means that they cannot be divided into rational and small enough units to be sold on a market to individual consumers."

Analysis Whatever "rational" means here, it can't be one of the senses given above.

Example 5 Is it rational to expect among the trading classes any high sense of justice, honour, or integrity, if the law enables men who act in this manner [declare bankruptcy] to shuffle off the consequences of their misconduct upon those who have been so unfortunate to trust them; and practically proclaims that it looks upon insolvency thus produced, as a 'misfortune', not an offence?

J. S. Mill, *Principles of Political Economy*

Analysis The uses we described of the term "rational" in economics started only in the twentieth century. Mill, writing in 1871, is using the term "rational" as people still do in ordinary speech.

Example 6 "One condition common to virtually all theories in economics is usually expressed by the use of the Latin phrase *ceteris paribus*. This roughly means 'let everything else be equal' or 'holding everything else constant'. In trying to assess the effect of one variable on another, we must isolate their relationship from other events that might also influence the situation that the theory tries to explain or predict."

Analysis Models and theories are used to reason by analogy. They are expected to apply when the differences don't matter. **Ceteris paribus** is an economist's way of saying that we are abstracting our model to just these "variables", and so long as all else is negligible—that is, the differences don't matter—the conclusion should be true.

Example 7 "A fundamental law of demand can now be restated: (1) "The demand (schedule) for any good is a negative relationship between price and amount." Or: (2) "The higher the price, the smaller the rate of consumption." More elaborately: (3) "Whatever the quantity of any good consumed at a particular price, a sufficiently higher price will induce any person to consume less." Or: (4) "Any person's consumption rate for any good will be increased (decreased) if the price is lowered (raised) sufficiently."

. . . [The law of demand as (4)] is an invention to describe the behavior of people in the real world. The present proposition of demand is a law simply because it describes a universal, verified truth about people's consumption and market behavior."

Analysis These statements of the law of demand are not equivalent: (1) is the usual version taking it to be a correlation; (3) and (4) are general causal claims; (2) can be understood as either causal or a correlation.

Is (4) "a universal verified truth about people's consumption and market behavior"? Many studies, both psychological and in the marketplace, show many kinds of situations in which (4) is false. *The law of demand is not a universal claim about human behavior, but an assumption of economists' models and theories*: When it is true (for the most part)—that is, when the differences don't matter—the model can be applied.

These assumptions of economics are often criticized: We all know from experience, and it's been confirmed by many psychological experiments, that most of the time, most people do not satisfy the conditions to be rational in the sense that economists use that term. So how can models based on the assumption that people are rational be good?

We saw in Section 5.2 that a good model need not have realistic assumptions. Models are analogies. That the assumption of rationality is clearly false much of the time is no criticism. *The key to judging a model is whether we can trace its path of abstraction in order to modify its assumptions when it gives bad predictions*.

With models based on assuming that people are rational, this has been done. Many economists now factor into their calculations that people can have motives other than maximizing profit. This is difficult to do, for many such motives cannot be measured in terms of money. How much would you pay to retain your right not to be put into slavery?

Some economists recognize that even when it is profit that motivates us, we might stop with decisions that give us "good enough" profit rather than trying to maximize. They replace maximizing with what they call *satisficing*.

Some economists note that people normally don't have all the information about a subject available to them, and in any case they don't have time to use all of it. The kinds of models they devise are based on what they call *bounded rationality*.

Some economists recognize that when their models make bad predictions, the problem may be in assuming that people have fixed preferences. They try to revise their models to take into account that Dick might prefer to buy a car rather than a pickup, and a pickup rather than an SUV, but after seeing an ad on TV, he prefers an SUV to both a pickup or car.

The one aspect of models based on assumptions of rationality that economists do not try to revise, however, is that people reason correctly. This is because the assumption that people reason correctly is not descriptive; it's not an abstraction. The rules for reasoning correctly are prescriptive, setting out how people should reason.

Rather than revise these assumptions, some economists try to devise models that are not based on the assumption of rationality at all. The interaction of people is crucial in determining what happens in economic situations, such economists claim. Those interactions and their influences are random, so predictions about what a particular person will do tomorrow, or what the stock market will do next week, cannot be made. However, the models these economists devise do make predictions about long-term trends of how people and markets behave—predictions that are statistical rather than causal. To give a full description of the assumptions behind their models would take too much space here, but we can give you an idea of what their work is like from a popular expositor of their views.

> [Alan] Kirman gives a model where . . . we have two types of operators in the financial markets, who look at different kinds of evidence to judge whether to buy or to sell. He provides completely realistic descriptions of these two types of agents. First, fundamentalists . . . hold that prices are essentially determined by their underlying, fundamental values. Second, chartists . . . believe that charts of the previous movements of the price of a currency or share over time provide evidence about its future behaviour. The techniques they use vary, from almost mystical mutterings about 'head and shoulders'. . . to the most advanced rocket science mathematics. But they form a view of future prices by extrapolating from past movements.
>
> These two approaches to prices will often give quite different opinions about what the price of any given asset ought to be. In 1984, a fundamentalist thought that a sharp fall in the dollar ought to take place. But a chartist expected it to stay high, simply because it had been high in the recent past.
>
> The essence of Kirman's model is that in any given period an agent can continue to behave in the same way as before; he or she can change behaviour independently in reaction to news; or the agent can be persuaded to switch by the behaviour of others—by the trails they leave when their buy or sell decisions appear on the dealing screens. . . .
>
> [T]he split between the number of dealers in any given asset who are either fundamentalists or chartists will change continuously. Sometimes almost everyone will be a chartist, but a switch back to the complete opposite at some point is inevitable. The very nature of the dynamics of the process dictates that some of these large changes will be very rapid. And, at these times, we are likely to see a large change in the price of the relevant asset, as it switches from being determined by fundamentals, say, to being generated by extrapolation of its own past behaviour as chartists come to dominate this particular market. In short, asset prices will be volatile because of the underlying volatility of the proportions of

different types of agents operating in the market. This is reinforced by the speed with which information is made available and exchanged in financial markets, so there is a very large number of 'meetings' with other agents. . . . Information on the activities of others bombards the dealer continuously.

Both [the efficient markets theory built on the assumption of rationality and Kirman's model] imply that changes in asset prices are essentially unpredictable, which appears to be true. But orthodox economics [the efficient markets theory] cannot account for the sheer volatility of asset markets, and the paradoxes which arise, such as traders continuing to buy assets which they say are over-valued.   Paul Ormerod, *Butterfly Economics*

The methods of critical thinking you have learned here should help you evaluate such reasoning and compare and understand the nature of the models you will encounter in your study of economics.

Index

Richard L. Epstein received his B.A. *summa cum laude* at the University of Pennsylvania and his Ph.D. in Mathematics at the University of California, Berkeley. He held a postdoctoral fellowship in mathematics and philosophy at Victoria University of Wellington, New Zealand before an extensive career teaching mathematics and philosophy. He has been a Fulbright Scholar to Brazil and a National Academy of Sciences Scholar to Poland. He also owned and managed the *Dog & Duck Coffee House*. He is the author of the series of research texts *The Semantic Foundations of Logic* as well as *Critical Thinking* and *Five Ways of Saying "Therefore"*. Currently he is head of the Advanced Reasoning Forum in Socorro, New Mexico.

Carolyn Kernberger received her B.G.S. *cum laude* from New Mexico Tech and her M.A. in Teaching English as a Second Language at the University of New Mexico. She has taught in the United States, Japan, and at the College of Micronesia FSM, where she was also the Accreditation Officer.

The authors are grateful to Troels Krøyer, Spokesman for Economics and Finance for the European Union (1990–1995), Peter Adams, Editor for Economics, and Steve Joos, Development Editor at South-Western/Thomson Learning for their many useful suggestions and conversations that helped shape this book.

Advanced Reasoning Forum
Imagine the Possibilities

http://www.AdvancedReasoningForum.org